To dear Beverly,

Hope you enjoy this charming book.

Love,
Mhim. × × ×

Christmas 1990.

Town House, Country House

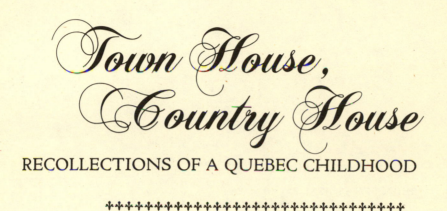

Town House, Country House

RECOLLECTIONS OF A QUEBEC CHILDHOOD

✦✦✦✦✦✦✦✦✦✦✦✦✦✦✦✦✦✦✦✦✦✦✦✦✦✦✦✦✦✦✦

HAZEL BOSWELL

EDITED BY
R.H. HUBBARD

ILLUSTRATED BY
JEAN-FRANÇOIS BÉLISLE

McGill-Queen's University Press
Montreal & Kingston • London • Buffalo

© McGill-Queen's University Press 1990

ISBN 0-7735-0721-3

Legal deposit third quarter 1990

Bibliothèque nationale du Québec

Printed in Canada

Canadian Cataloguing in Publication Data

Boswell, Hazel, 1882-1979
Town house, country house
ISBN 0-7735-0721-3
1. Children – Quebec (Province) – Fiction.
I. Hubbard, R. H. (Robert Hamilton), 1916-
II. Bélisle, Jean-François III. Title.
PS8553.O89T6 1990 jC813'.54 C90-090260-4
PZ7.B68To 1990

Contents

Preface

THE AUTHOR, HAZEL DE LOTBINIÈRE BOS-
well (1882–1979), had already published two
books before she completed the manuscript for
this one. These two were *French Canada* (1938)
and *Legends of Quebec* (1966). Both were illustrated with her own water-colour drawings in a
sprightly folk-art style.

She was the daughter of one of the principal
characters of this book, Julie, the eldest of the
seven surviving children of Sir Henri (1829–
1908) and Lady Joly de Lotbinière. In 1882, Julie
married St George Boswell. Their daughters
Hazel and Olive never married but lived quietly
in Quebec all their lives.

Julie's brothers and sisters, the 'big family'
of the story, are listed in the Introduction by

✦✦✦

their nicknames. More formally they were Edmond (1859–1911), Matilda (1860–1902), Margaretta (1861–1949), Alain (1862–1944), Ethel (1865–1935) and Henri-Gustave (1866–1960). Edmond inherited the Seigneury of Lotbinière while his brothers followed careers in the British army. The girls all married, two of them in England.

The family, whose original surname was Chartier, was an old and distinguished one, traceable to fourteenth-century Dijon. Over the centuries its members became landowners and seigneurs, their most famous scion being René-Pierre Chartier de Lotbinière who in the early seventeenth century was a professor of surgery in Paris and the favourite doctor of Louis XIII. It was a younger son of his who, in 1651, came to Canada with *his* young son. This latter, in turn soldier and chief counsellor of New France, became first Seigneur of Lotbinière on the St Lawrence in 1672. The rest of the family saga is outlined in the Introduction.

The old city of Quebec, scene of the earlier chapters of the book, had been the capital of New France since its founding by Samuel de Champlain in 1608. It remained the seat of the

+++

Governor General of British North America after the British Conquest of 1759–60, and though it was periodically abandoned as the capital of United Canada from 1841 to 1867, the Governors General maintained a residence there. By the time of the story, presumably autumn 1872 to summer 1873 (Hazel Boswell dated it 1872), the city had been the capital of the province of Quebec since Confederation five years previously. Its old families, including the de Lotbinières, lived in comfortable houses within the walls of the upper town, the site also of the Parliament building, the Roman Catholic and Anglican cathedrals, the Governor's Garden, the Séminaire, and the Ursuline Convent – in the last two of which respectively the boys and Julie attended school. In the lower town and on the slopes leading to the upper were huddled the shops, houses, and markets described in the Christmas chapter of Boswell's story. To the east of the city, on the north shore, was that cynosure for both residents and visitors, the Falls of Montmorency, beyond which was the sugar bush visited by the children.

By the early 1870s seigneurial tenure with its apparatus of dues and privileges had been

✠✠✠✠✠✠✠✠✠✠✠✠✠✠✠✠✠✠✠✠✠✠✠✠✠✠✠✠✠✠✠✠✠✠✠✠✠✠✠

dismantled for just over a decade. The seigneurs, however, remained the owners of large areas of land and were the occupants of the manor houses; they were still addressed as Seigneur even though they no longer held the power or privilege their parents or grandparents had enjoyed. Because of the strong British presence in Quebec, intermarriage between French- and English-speaking families was common. It was thus not unusual for a seigneurial family like the Jolys to be anglophone or bilingual but of French descent.

As Hazel Boswell tells us, the de Lotbinière Seigneury was a large estate between Quebec and Trois-Rivières on the south shore of the St Lawrence River on which the tenant farmers were served by grist and saw mills owned by the Seigneur. The manor house had been built by the first Joly in the early years of the nineteenth century, replacing an older and smaller one nearer the village of Lotbinière. Behind the manor house were a 'Gothick' hen house and other outbuildings, and around it stretched gardens and orchards. A road led up to it from a jetty on the point, where the side-wheeled steamers put in on their criss-crossings of the St Lawrence, carrying passengers, livestock, and produce to and from Quebec. The beach around Pointe-Platon was the scene of the children's picnics and their discovery of the derelict boat.

On the high ground behind the manor house, roads led off to Lotbinière with its fine big church, to several hamlets, and on to the saw-mill on the Rivière du Chêne. In summer the countryside was a northern Arcadia peopled by kindly and industrious folk well endowed with native wit and folk-legend.

Towards the end of her life Hazel Boswell entrusted the manuscript of this book to her cousin of a younger generation, Madeleine de Lotbinière Widawska. Madeleine made a few revisions, chiefly in the matter of substituting real names for Hazel's fictitious ones, but she had not succeeded in finding a publisher by the time I visited her several years ago in company with her brother Edmond Joly de Lotbinière. As soon as I read this endearing narrative of life in Victorian French Canada, I was sure that it would appeal to many people both young and old. My own part as editor has been restricted to elim-inating the occasional repetitions of a writer in her nineties and to smoothing out the narrative, while preserving the liveliness of the writing. (I

✠✠

have also left in the text certain details, such as the parlour car in the final chapter, that seem to reflect Hazel's own childhood memories rather than those of her mother.) In the process I gained an appreciation of a family of charm and cultivation which over the centuries has contributed much to its province and nation.

My warmest thanks go to Madeleine and to my old friends Edmond and his wife Francine for their interest in and support of my efforts. To the members of the McGill-Queen's University Press I owe a debt of gratitude for their sympathy and care during the process of publication.

R.H.H.

Introduction

THIS IS THE STORY OF A YEAR IN THE LIVES of my mother and her brothers and sisters when they were children. I have pieced it together from the tales my mother told me long ago. In winter the family lived in their house in the city of Quebec and in summer they all went to the manor house on their old seigneury in the country.

The Seigneury of Lotbinière was a large tract of land forty miles up the St Lawrence River from Quebec, on the south shore. It had been granted by King Louis XIV of France to our ancestor René-Louis Chartier de Lotbinière who arrived in New France in the early days of the colony. One of his descendants was made a Marquis by King Louis XVI just before the French Revolution. His son, the second Marquis, left his estates in Canada to his only

✦✦

children, three girls who were so tall and thin that they were nicknamed *les trois canelles* – the 'Three Cinnamon Sticks.' One of these girls, named Julie, inherited the Seigneury of Lotbinière and married a young Swiss, Gustave Joly. And that is how the Seigneury came into the Joly family.

My grandfather on my mother's side was the son of Gustave and Julie and began life as plain Henri-Gustave Joly. That was still his name in 1872, the year in which this story takes place. At that time he was a Member of Parliament but was soon to become Prime Minister of the Province of Quebec. Later he officially assumed the name of de Lotbinière and eventually, after being knighted by Queen Victoria as Sir Henri Joly de Lotbinière, was appointed Lieutenant Governor of the Province of British Columbia.

He and my grandmother, née Margaretta Gowen, had ten children, seven of whom lived beyond infancy. The eldest of those who survived was my mother, Julie, who at the time of the story was fourteen. Then came the dignified Edmond who was thirteen, the sensible Tilly of twelve, the temperamental Mic of eleven, the brave Alain of ten, the impulsive Ethel of seven, and last of all the lively but already philosophical Henri of six. You will hear a great deal of all of them in this story.

So you see it was a big family. And besides the children's parents there also lived with them my grandfather's blind cousin, whom everyone called 'Tante' Mathilde, and his younger brother – that is to say Oncle Édouard lived there whenever he was

on leave from the army. It was he who supplied the element of high romance in the children's lives. He was an officer in the British army and at this time was stationed in India. He told thrilling tales of elephants and tigers and of rajahs who sliced off their enemies' heads with a single stroke of their scimitars. But the most romantic thing Oncle Édouard ever did was to bury his horse in the very tomb which

Alexander the Great had built in north India for his favourite steed, Bucephalus. Oncle Édouard often told exciting stories of Alexander's conquests in ancient times.

Tante Mathilde, in spite of her blindness, was the expert knitter of endless quantities of long red stockings for the children, as well as winter mitts and long woollen scarves that were so light that they floated round the girls' heads and so were called 'clouds.'

Then there were the servants who were needed to look after such a large family. The children's nurse, Mary Ann Doyle, was very Irish and was better liked by their mother than by them. Mary Ann believed in forestalling naughtiness or, in her own words, 'taking time by the forelock.' That meant that when they were dressed and ready to join the grown-ups downstairs she would give each one what she called a 'bother' on the ear to make sure ahead of time that they would behave.

There were also Mary Ann's niece Yvonne, the housemaid, Rosalie the cook, Narcisse the coachman, and of course Jumbo, the big Newfoundland dog who lived in the stables with Narcisse. But the children's great favourite was the butler whom everyone

called Beau-Charles because he was so handsome.
Indeed, next to their parents, whom of course they
had to love more than anyone else in the world, and
their soldier uncle and Tante Mathilde, they loved
Beau-Charles best of all. Perhaps it was because he
was a sort of grown-up child, and because he in his
turn loved them all very dearly.

As I have already told you, the family spent
their winters in Quebec, and so now I must tell you
a little about their house in that old walled city which
was the ancient capital of Canada. Like so many
other old houses there, it was built of grey stone
and it stood in the very last street below the hill that
rises steeply up to the Citadel on the summit of Cape
Diamond. The Citadel is a great fortress that dom-
inates the whole city and guards the narrows of the
St Lawrence River. Every winter the river froze solid
and a road was made across the ice to the town of
Lévis on the opposite shore.

The proper name for a slope leading up to a
fort is a glacis. Now when the children were young
they didn't know what this meant or even how it was
spelt, and so they thought of it the way it was pro-
nounced: a Glass Sea. Perhaps some children in
Quebec still call it that. Across from their house a

✠✠✠

brown picket fence separated the glacis from the street, and when they climbed over it they had a perfect playground in summer and a perfect hill for sliding and building snow forts in winter. When they looked up to the Citadel they could see the wind-whipped flag flying from the highest redoubt, and they could always hear the noon gun boom out over the city.

The family's summer home was called Platon, which is the French name for the ancient Greek philosopher Plato. It was the manor house of the Seigneury and nestled into the hillside overlooking Pointe-Platon which jutted out into the St Lawrence. In those days there weren't any motor cars, so the family travelled there in a paddle-wheel steamer.

And now I take up the story just where my mother always began.

At Home and at School in Quebec

IT WAS SO EARLY IN THE MORNING THAT DAY in September that the breakfast dishes weren't even cleared away. The younger children – Tilly, Mic, Ethel, and Henri – all had their noses pressed against the dining room window. What they were watching was their friend Beau-Charles being hustled down the street by a big policeman named Constable O'Rourke accompanied by Oncle Édouard. The butler was trying his best to bite the hand that held him: not that he wanted to hurt it, but when he'd had what he called his *petit coup* – his little drop of whisky – he did things he was very sorry for afterwards.

This was by no means the first time it had happened. Whenever Beau-Charles yielded to temptation Mr O'Rourke had to take him off to the police

✦✦✦

station. To tell you the truth, the children were glad, because every time Beau-Charles took his dram he would be very easy on them and let them dip their fingers into the honey pot or the jam pot, lick them, and put them back in for more. As he did his work in the pantry he would sing beautiful sad songs and tears would roll down his cheek. At first the singing was soft but as the *petit coup* took effect it became

louder and louder. It was then that Mr O'Rourke would have to come for him.

Father was always upset when this happened. He would pace up and down the drawing room carpet, pausing every few steps to exclaim to Mother, 'This is the last time, positively the last!' But the children knew better, because Beau-Charles always came back and Father never dismissed him. In fact they eagerly looked forward to his return because he always brought with him a big cake with white icing on which was written in pink sugar letters the single word *Pardon*. And that was what happened this very day, and Beau-Charles was once more forgiven.

The older children – Julie and her brothers Alain and Edmond – went to boarding school in Quebec. Julie was at the old Ursuline Convent and only came home on Thursdays, because in those days children had their holiday then instead of on Saturday. Edmond and Alain attended the ancient Séminaire de Québec near the Cathedral and wore its smart uniform, a dark blue frock coat with white piping, a green knitted sash, and a cap with a shiny black peak.

Before I come to Julie's adventure at the convent I must tell you a little of what she was like as a girl. She had a vivid imagination and told the younger children many wonderful stories. She had a talent for make-believe, which came out most strongly at picnics when she would dress the others up as wood fairies and make them parasols out of fronds of bracken. At other times, when her brothers and sisters got into fights with other children, she would defend them fiercely. 'I am Helen Mac-Gregor!' she would exclaim. 'Now come on!' And when she was Helen MacGregor no one dared to attack her, even the biggest boys. You see, pretending to be someone else made her feel very brave, and

✦✦✦✦✦✦✦✦✦✦✦✦✦✦✦✦✦✦✦✦✦✦✦✦✦✦✦✦✦✦✦✦✦✦✦✦✦✦

Helen MacGregor was the fearless heroine of Sir Walter Scott's book *Rob Roy*.

But when Julie first went to the convent she cried a great deal because she was lonely and missed her family very much. She even missed Mary Ann. In those first weeks she was always getting into trouble because the life of a boarder in a convent school was so strange to her.

The worst of her troubles came on the evening of her first bath away from home. To her great surprise the Sister in charge of the bathroom asked her for her bathing dress. Julie had no such thing with her, having at the end of the summer left her only one in the country. She also told the Sister she couldn't for the life of her think why you needed one away from the beach. The Sister exclaimed that *she* couldn't understand how a *mère chrétienne* – a good Christian mother like yours and mine – could think of sending her little girl to school without a proper dress to cover her up in the bath. And so the nun began searching among Julie's clothes for something that would do and at last came up with a starched white petticoat. It was Julie's best petticoat, with lace round its frilled hem, and she didn't want it to get wet. But as she left the room the Sister

told Julie to undress and tie the waist of the petticoat up round her neck.

So Julie, like the obedient girl she was, got into this peculiar costume. It wasn't easy to take a bath in. When the starch melted there seemed to be a great deal more petticoat than when it was dry. It stuck to her arms and legs and even got into her mouth. Finally, after much struggling with it, she slipped out of it and hung it over the edge of the bath. Then at last she could enjoy her bath. Indeed she splashed about so noisily that she didn't hear the Sister rapping on the door. The first thing she did hear was the nun's shriek of horror at seeing Julie in the nude. She even slammed the door behind her as she escaped, and that is something no one must ever do in a convent, let alone a nun.

The next day Julie was given a solemn lecture on modesty and obedience. But she wasn't punished because she hadn't known what a dreadful thing it was she had done. Nonetheless she cried a good deal until one of the girls in her class told her she had often taken off her bathing dress in the bath and had only been caught once. This friend went on to say that though she'd been sent off to chapel to confess to the *bon Père*, the priest had only given her a light penance to do. So it couldn't have been a very bad sin of the kind called a *péché mortel* – a mortal sin.

At home, when Julie told her story, Father and Mother said she mustn't worry because she had only made a mistake. Mother had a lovely bathing dress made for her and sent the Sister a beautiful cake. So everything turned out all right.

Her brother Alain's troubles, when he first went to the Séminaire, were more serious than hers. He was an excellent shot with his catapult, which he always carried with him, and could hit nearly anything he chose. One day, in the interval between lessons, a friend of his pointed up to a row of statues of the

saints standing on a ledge running round the class-
room.

'I bet you can't knock the head off one of
those.'

'I bet I can knock them all off,' boasted Alain.

All the rest of the class joined in. 'Let's see
you do it,' they shouted.

Alain's blood was up. He took out the catapult,
put a small stone in it and took aim. Off flew the
head of one saint. The more the others egged him
on, the more saints lost their heads. Just as the last
one was being beheaded, and the boys were shouting
'Bravo!,' the door opened and in walked their school-
master. When he saw the damage done to the saints
he gave the whole class a stern lecture and kept them
all in after school. Alain and his friend he kept in
even later and gave them canings and notes to take
home to their fathers.

When Alain produced his note, Father put on
a very sad and disapproving face, just as he had done
when Beau-Charles was arrested. He told Alain he
had disgraced the family and then took him off to
the study for more whacks. After two punishments
in one day Alain found it pretty painful to sit down
and had to do his homework standing up. Everyone,

✠✠✠

including Mary Ann, felt sorry for him, and just before bed she rubbed his bottom with her favourite liniment made of turkey oil and camphor.

' 'Twill ease,' she said, 'though the good Lord only knows you don't deserve to be eased, bringing grief and disgrace to a decent family as you have.'

Alain felt ashamed of himself. He was forbidden ever to take his catapult to school again and his pocket money was stopped to pay for repairs to the saints. But he remained a hero to his classmates. Even the *professeur* didn't seem to bear him any ill will.

Autumn Adventures

IT WAS A LOVELY AUTUMN AFTERNOON IN the Governor's Garden in Upper Town Quebec. This quiet green park with its tall trees is just behind the terrace that overlooks Lower Town and the broad St Lawrence. The sky was a bright blue, the air crisp and cool. The lawns were strewn with red and yellow leaves, some of which had been raked up into great heaps.

Tilly, Mic, Ethel, and Henri were playing around the monument to Wolfe and Montcalm that stands in the middle of the garden. With them were several of their cousins and friends, along with their nurses and Jumbo the dog. Now Jumbo loved a game of tag every bit as much as the children did, but suddenly he uttered a loud bark and dashed off. The children stopped their game to see what had so

✛✛

excited him and saw him rushing up to someone coming down the path. It was Barney O'Shea.

They all knew Barney pretty well, and that was because he wasn't at all like anyone else they knew. Mary Ann said he was 'queer in the head' but they never understood quite what that meant. His head looked for all the world like anyone else's; but of course you couldn't see inside it, and that was where Mary Ann meant he was queer. Occasionally he would walk about brandishing a stick and muttering, 'Out of my way, get out of my way!' At times like these it was best not even to talk to him because he might get angry and chase you. Once upon a time he had been a soldier and to prove this he proudly wore on his chest the shiny round tops of several tobacco tins hanging from bits of green ribbon. 'My Waterloo medals,' he called them, though he would have had to be very old to have fought under Wellington at the Battle of Waterloo nearly sixty years earlier. At any rate, he now spent a great deal of his time in the garden because Mr O'Neill the gardener was always friendly to him.

Well, at this particular moment Mr O'Shea was wheeling his friend's barrow along the path. When he came to the monument he set it down under a big elm tree near by. The children gathered round as he slowly took off his coat and folded it up.

'Why are you doing that?' asked Henri who was curious about everything.

'Because I am about to retire to my bed,' he replied in his grandest tone of voice.

At this moment Mary Ann saw what was going on and called the children to her. At the best of times she didn't like them talking to Mr O'Shea. As for the most part they were obedient children, they ran to the bench where she was sitting with Nanou, their cousins' quick little French nurse, and Margaret Cameron, who was the nurse of their friend Christopher Dawson.

'Haven't I told you not to be talking to him?' she demanded.

'But he says he's going to bed,' Henri explained, 'and he's starting to undress.'

'Going to bed!' snorted Mary Ann. 'He can't go to bed in a public place. It isn't decent.' And so saying she got up and bore down on Mr O'Shea, who was now taking off one of his shoes. He had big holes in his socks and his toes stuck out through them.

In her sternest voice she asked him, 'Whatever are you doing, taking off your coat and shoes on a bitter day like this?'

✦✦

'I'm retiring to bed in this commodious coffin,' replied Mr O'Shea with as much dignity as he could summon, and pointing to the wheelbarrow. 'And nobody asked you to kiss me good-night either, grandma.' Then he stood up, angrily shaking his shoe at her and shouting, 'And what's more, madam, I'm not sharing my bed with any cross-eyed old harridan. So begone!'

Mary Ann's face was scarlet as she caught Tilly and Mic by the hand and hurried them back to the bench. But because she had only two hands, Henri and Ethel were left behind, puzzling out how Mr O'Shea could possibly go to bed in a wheelbarrow with no sheets or pillows.

Mary Ann burst out to Margaret and Nanou: 'Faith, it's true he's set his heart on going to bed here! He'll be stripped to the pelt before you know it.'

✦✦

'I'll go and fetch Mr O'Neill,' said Nanou, folding up the crochet work she was doing and putting it into her bag. She scurried off to find the gardener as fast as her short legs could carry her. Now Nanou was quite the nicest nurse anyone could ever hope to have, and the children secretly wished they could exchange Mary Ann for her. She wore a cap of checked silk ribbon with wide streamers that hung down behind to the hem of her dress, the sort of cap nurses wore in France, where she came from. She was the smallest grown-up you ever saw. Mother once told the children that Nanou had been such a tiny baby that when her parents took her to church to be christened they put her into her grandmother's muff to keep her warm.

In a moment Nanou came tripping back with Mr O'Neill at her heels, and following him was the lad who helped in the garden. Mr O'Neill was hastily pulling on his coat as he walked, because Nanou had caught him just as he was having his 'bit of a bite.' He was tall and thin, with a middle that didn't curve out like most men's but in like the string of a violin bow. He had a long drooping moustache and quite the bluest eyes you ever saw. He went straight up to Mr O'Shea.

'Hey, Barney,' he said, 'what's this about going to bed and wasting a grand day like this?'

His friend stopped in the middle of taking off his other shoe, looked up and politely replied, 'You're right as ever. It's a grand day for sure.' It was as if he'd forgotten all about going to bed.

'You come along with me, Barney,' Mr O'Neill continued. 'I've got something for you up there at the shed as will make the two eyes in your head dance for joy.'

'Would it be sweet Molly Malone, now?' asked Mr O'Shea with some considerable interest.

'You just come along and see with your own eyes what I've got for you up there,' said the gardener.

So Mr O'Shea got up, put on his shoes and coat and gave a smart military salute. 'At your service, sir,' he said, and began to sing 'Cockles and mussels! alive, alive, oh!' Mr O'Neill led him up the path with the lad and the wheelbarrow bringing up the rear. The children never did find out what was in the shed.

Mary Ann rose. 'Faith, it was a good thing Mr O'Neill was here to distract him,' she said, 'for he was set on stripping down to the skin. It's time to go home.' The children at once began picking up their toys because they knew from the tone of her voice there would be trouble if they didn't obey — even worse trouble than not having strawberry jam for tea.

Some little time later came the *Fête de Sainte-Catherine*. There was to be a party because children in Quebec always had one on that day. Everyone eagerly looked forward to this party because it was the special day for *la tire* — toffee pulling — and next

to Christmas it was the best party of the year. You pulled molasses toffee, ducked for apples, and played games like the Mulberry Bush, Oranges and Lemons, and Musical Chairs.

On the evening of the great day, as soon as dinner had ended, preparations for the party began. The girls put on their second-best plaid dresses and pinafores, and Mary Ann gave them ribbons for their hair instead of the usual combs. She also gave them a final warning in the nursery: 'Now mind and behave

✦✦✦✦✦✦✦✦✦✦✦✦✦✦✦✦✦✦✦✦✦✦✦✦✦✦✦✦✦✦✦✦✦✦✦✦✦✦✦

yourselves and don't disgrace your pa and ma or me.
Remember you are Christian children of good family
and not ignorant young heathens.' Then she opened
the door and they sedately trooped out.

Once out of Mary Ann's sight they raced down
to the kitchen, which was presided over by their great
good friend Rosalie the cook. Fat and good-natured,

she never scolded them no matter what they did. She
always allowed them to sit at her kitchen table and
scrape out the bowls and lick the spoons.

Rosalie was getting ready for *la tire*. Helped by
her niece Yvonne, she set out two big iron pots and
took down from a shelf a brown crockery jar of

molasses and another of *cassonade* – brown sugar –
carefully measuring out so much to each pot and
then adding big slabs of butter. Then she put the
pots on the stove to boil. After that Yvonne brought
out plates, buttered them, and put them in the *dépense*
– the pantry – to be ready for the toffee when it
was cooked. But by this time the guests had begun
to arrive, and so the children ran upstairs to greet
them.

It was always a big party, and this year was no
exception. All the cousins and their mothers and
nurses came, and a good many friends too. First of
all there was a wonderful tea of bread and butter
with strawberry jam, pink jellies, cakes, *charlotte russe*,
cream puffs, and little sugar lambs. The lambs were
white with pink eyes and each sat on a macaroon.
Finally there was ribbon candy, pink and yellow barley-sugar fishes, and, at the very end, crackers to
pull.

After tea everyone went down to the kitchen.
Yvonne and Beau-Charles brought out the pots in
which the toffee was cooling. Rosalie set a bowl of
flour on the table and made everyone, children and
grown-ups alike, dip both hands in it so that the
candy wouldn't stick to them when they pulled it.

Then all three servants folded the toffee into big balls and put one on each plate.

Everyone began pulling furiously. Now even when toffee is still soft it is delicious, and the children couldn't wait to pop bits into their mouths. Sometimes loose ends fell to the floor but before these could make a mess Rosalie and Yvonne picked them up and patted them into tidy coils. While Henri's *tire* was soft he pulled off quite a big piece, and when no one was looking he and his cousin Paul Savage gave it to Tante Mathilde's Persian cat Omar. Omar snatched it up as eagerly as you would expect of a big greedy cat. But when he began to chew the toffee it stuck to his teeth and he flew into a rage. In trying to dislodge it with his paws he only succeeded in getting them stuck as well.

Mary Ann's eagle eye spotted this and she grew very angry. 'If it wasn't the holy Saint's own birthday,' she cried, 'I'd take you fine larribucks (her Irish word for young rowdies) and warm your hides for you.' As it turned out, Yvonne took Omar on her knee and cleaned his mouth and paws. He allowed her to do this for him because he was fond of her – and that was because it was she who gave him his meals. Cats, like people, know the right ones to be friends with.

After everyone had eaten as much of the *tire* as possible, the dancing began to the music of Narcisse's accordion. Father and Oncle Édouard came downstairs and danced with the children's nurses. Beau-Charles and Mary Ann together performed a lively jig. Finally all present joined hands, formed a big circle, and sang the old good-night song, '*Bon soir, mes amis, bon soir.*' And that was how the party ended.

A Quebec Christmas

JULIE AND HER TWO ELDER BROTHERS HAD nice long Christmas holidays. These they enjoyed to the fullest because winter is a wonderful season in the city of Quebec, with shiny blue skies and streets dazzlingly white with snow. The roofs too were white and fringed with icicles hanging from the eaves and window-sills. The air was alive with the sound of sleigh bells. The horses all had strings of bells attached to their harnesses. Some of them, the very grandest of all, had little silver bells on their ears and saddles as well.

Every day of the week before Christmas the streets were busy with wood sleighs full of Christmas trees. As the horses plodded through, their drivers went from door to door ringing the bell and asking whether the *patron* – the master of the house – wanted

✳✳✳

✦✦✦

a tree. Many families bought theirs this way, but the younger Joly children always went to Christmas market with Mother and chose one from Madame Claveau. She was from Jeune-Lorette, a little village where the Huron Indians lived, and was small and solid and had a face as round and rosy as an apple. She wore a black coat reaching down to her knees and a black woollen hood held in place with a grey scarf. Under the coat was a linen apron with a huge pocket from which she made change. The children thought she must be very rich indeed to keep such handfuls of pennies and silver coins in that pocket.

On the day before Christmas, Madame Claveau's little red sleigh stood beside a clump of Christmas trees she had stuck into the snow, making the place look for all the world like the edge of a wood. While Mother was buying chickens as well as *boudin* – blood sausage – half a pig, and all the other things one needs at Christmas, Madame Claveau's son 'Bébé' helped the children to choose a tree.

After this they toured the whole market-place. So many sleighs were drawn up in double lines that the lanes between them looked like little streets running all the way from the stone market hall down to the bottom of the square. But unlike real streets with houses, these were lined with sleighs back to back

✝✝✝

so that you could see everything in them. Behind them the horses faced each other, some with nose-bags attached to their ears, others eating bundles of hay on the snow. All of them wore bits of *catalogne* – rag rug – over their backs to keep them warm, but in spite of these they looked very cold and sad. Clusters of Christmas trees sprouted everywhere from the snow. It was plain for all to see that this was Christmas market.

Next Mother took the children to Mr McGuire's bakery. This was a famous little shop with a steep roof and huge chimneys in old Quebec style, and in it you could buy the best hot buns in all the world. To go inside you went down two steps from street-level and pushed the door open. Then you were in a big square room with a pot-bellied stove in the middle, its little mica window aglow from the flames within. This was the ideal place to dry your wet mitts while savouring Mr McGuire's buns. Mother also bought each child a gingerbread horse to take home, for the shop was just as famous for these as for its buns.

Then came Christmas Eve and the excitement of going on a secret shopping expedition with Father. Mother stayed at home because of course she knew they were going to buy her a Christmas present which must be a surprise. While they were out, Mother and Tante Mathilde and Mary Ann busied themselves making the rooms ready for Santa Claus's visit that night and the big party the following evening. Then they packed big baskets full of Christmas dinners to be sent out to needy families.

Each week of the year up to Christmas the younger children had received ten cents as pocket money, and the older ones twenty-five. Each one had a bank for Christmas shopping money. When they took the money out of the banks Father gave them each an extra dollar because there was never enough for all the gifts they had to buy.

When the presents had been bought and all the money spent, Father took the children to Mademoiselle Vidal's sweets shop as a climax to the whole day. It was on a street corner and, like the bakery, it had a steep roof and tall chimneys. It too was

famous for a speciality: 'saw logs' which were fat round sticks of molasses candy. You went in through a narrow door beside which was a low shop window full of red candy roosters and gold barley-sugar hens.

The short fat Mademoiselle Vidal welcomed the family like the old friends they were. She had once been their sewing maid but had longed to have a little shop of her own and had saved her every penny until she had money enough to buy it. The black dress she wore was exactly the same shape as she was, except for a skirt that was gathered in at the waist. Her bodice had a row of shiny buttons down the front and white lace at the collar and cuffs. Over the skirt she wore a black apron trimmed with black lace. Perched on her nose was a pair of gold-rimmed spectacles that had once belonged to her mother. The brown plait of hair round the back of her head was also inherited from her mother.

Every Christmas Eve she gave each child a huge red-and-white peppermint bull's-eye which was nice to suck on while they did the rest of the shopping. Then she set a tray of her roosters and hens on the counter and allowed each of them to choose one. She never minded how long they took to make their choices or how carefully they examined them, so long as they didn't lick them. That she would never allow.

On this particular Christmas Eve, when the choices were finally made, the children helped Father pick out things to hang on the tree as well as a peppermint stick each for Mary Ann and everyone else in the house and all the guests who were invited to the Christmas party.

Once everything was tied up and paid for, they said good-bye to Mademoiselle Vidal and set out for home. It was lovely to be out so late in the evening when the shop windows were lit up and the gas lamps at street corners shone like misty moons. Sleighs dashed by, filling the frosty air with the tinkle of bells. Buffalo robes flew out behind the drivers who, standing up in their big fur coats, looked like so many Santa Clauses, their whiskers fringed with tiny icicles. Little newsboys ran along the pavement with their bundles of papers, calling out, 'Paper, sir, evening paper?' Father always gave them pennies and wished them a happy Christmas but never took a paper.

When at last they came home there was the special treat of having tea in the dining room instead of the nursery. Mother sat at one end of the table brewing the tea and Mary Ann sat at the other presiding over a jug of chocolate. Oncle Édouard and Tante Mathilde and the other grown-ups sat

✦✦

down with them, so that it was a really big tea. Afterwards they helped to put up the tree, hung up their stockings on the nursery chimney-piece, and finally, with reluctance, went to bed.

When they woke up on Christmas morning it was to find the stockings bulging with presents, and these they set upon with breathless excitement. By

the time the breakfast gong sounded from the hall the nursery floor was littered with gifts, wrapping paper, and bits of string. It was the one day of the year when Mary Ann didn't make them tidy up before going downstairs.

Christmas breakfast was a substantial meal of sausage, cold ham, and baked potatoes. A thin brown sausage, curled round and round on its platter like a huge Bath bun, was proclaimed by Oncle Édouard

to be the best in the world. At the end of breakfast Beau-Charles brought in two great dishes of
steaming-hot popovers which, when filled with butter
and maple sugar, were simply delicious. After this
feast everyone went up to the nursery to admire the
presents – and then it was time to go to church.

In those days each family had its own pew in
church with its name on it. The Joly pew was a big
square one under a gallery and it was furnished with
red velvet cushions and hassocks. The inside walls
of the church were decorated with wreaths and stars
fashioned from evergreen boughs, and festoons of
green branches looped down from the ceiling to the
tops of the white pillars that supported the galleries.
The total effect was of a graceful arch over the whole
length of the centre aisle.

After church the family had lunch in the house
of the children's grandpapa and grandmamma. Then
they came home to play with their presents until it
was time to dress for dinner and the Christmas tree.
These festivities were attended by the grandparents
and even a great-grandparent or two, along with all
the uncles and aunts and cousins and a host of friends.
Beau-Charle's brother-in-law Théophile Auger, a
solemn-looking man, and Mademoiselle Philomène,

✢✢

an old friend of the children, came in to help with the serving.

For Philomène, this Christmas was a sad occasion because her mother had just died. Before taking off her outdoor clothes, she went to the nursery to show off her new mourning hat to Mary Ann. It was a very grand hat indeed, made of black crêpe and with a long veil reaching down to her waist. Mary Ann declared it the finest she had ever seen.

'Sure and it's fit for the Queen herself,' she added as she turned it round and round in her hands, 'and better than that little crown she's forever wearing on her head.' Mary Ann hadn't much use for Queen Victoria and wouldn't allow her picture to be hung in the nursery.

There were so many people at dinner that it took two tables to seat them. All the grown-ups except Oncle Édouard were at one and all the children and their uncle at the other. Each table had a little Christmas tree as its centre-piece and each was lit by two tall silver candlesticks. Father carved one turkey at his table and Oncle Édouard the other at the children's table. After the turkey came a *sorbet*, which is a kind of refreshing fruit ice eaten between courses, and then Beau-Charles and Théophile proudly bore in two big plum puddings, ablaze like bonfires, with sprigs of holly stuck into their tops.

But just as the puddings were being set down a commotion broke out in the hall. The next moment Philomène burst in sobbing, followed by Rosalie, Yvonne, and Mary Ann, all looking very frightened.

'Why, whatever is the matter?' asked Mother.

'It's Philomène's mother, ma'am,' exclaimed Mary Ann, 'came and looked at her through the kitchen window. Poor creature, she was burnt black as a cinder. 'Twas only a bit of her breast was left a natural white. 'Tis God alone knows the sins of each one of us, for she always passed in her life for a good woman if there ever was one.' At this last statement Mary Ann crossed herself fervently.

Everyone began quizzing Philomène. 'I was alone in the kitchen,' she gasped, 'and my dear mother came and looked at me through the window. She came to reproach me for taking part in these festivities whilst masses were still being said for her soul.' And she began sobbing all the harder.

'I'll go and see what it is,' said Oncle Édouard, 'It was probably someone trying to frighten her, or else burglars.'

All the other men got up and were followed into the hall by Alain and Edmond. The rest of the party made for the door too, even Mary Ann and

++

the children – for if one is brave he makes all the
rest brave too. So along the hall they trooped and
down the basement stairs.

In the brightly lit kitchen the tables were piled
high with dishes, and a lovely smell compounded of
turkey and sausage and coffee filled the air. And
outside the big window, standing on his hind legs
with his paws on the sill and his nose pressed to the
pane, the patch on his front very white in the glare
from the kitchen, was Jumbo! He was looking long-
ingly at all the delicious things to eat. Everyone burst
out laughing.

'Why, it's only Jumbo,' they cried.

'Where is Philomène?' asked Oncle Édouard.

Alain ran to find her, with Mother and Mary
Ann and the children hard on her heels. They found
her sitting wretchedly in the pantry with her apron
over her head and Yvonne and Beau-Charles and
Narcisse trying to comfort her.

'It was only Jumbo you saw, Philomène,' said
Alain.

'How can you mock me so, Monsieur Alain?'
she moaned. 'As if I didn't know my own mother
when I saw her!'

Mother took her by the hand. 'My poor Philomène,' she said, 'come and see for yourself.' And between them they led her to the kitchen. Someone had let Jumbo in and he was in the middle of the floor gobbling up a nice gristly bit of meat.

'See, it was Jumbo you saw looking in,' said Oncle Édouard.

'You're only saying that out of the goodness of your heart, to console me,' said Philomène, sobbing all the more, 'but I know it was my dear mother come to reproach me, *sans coeur que je suis*' – heartless as I am. Nothing could persuade her otherwise, and they had to leave her sitting dolefully in the kitchen with Mary Ann and Yvonne.

It was hard to settle down at table after all the excitement. But when Oncle Édouard began telling stories of India everyone was soon laughing and talking and eating plum pudding. When the tables were cleared, two huge dishes of 'snapdragon' were brought in and everyone grabbed for raisins and almonds from the blazing brandy. And then there were Christmas crackers to pull.

Last of all Father stood up at his place to perform his special Christmas Night trick. Beau-Charles brought him a lighted candle in a silver candlestick.

'Now,' said Father, 'watch me eat the candle.'

All the rest, children and grown-ups, watched him intently, though they all knew from past experience just what he was going to do. With due solemnity he took the candle and held it up for all to see.

'One, two, three,' he cried and popped it into his mouth, flame and all. No matter how many times the family had seen this, it still seemed a terrifying thing to do. They expected him to howl with pain; but all he did was to press his hand to his stomach and utter a very mild, 'Ouch!' How did he do it? The boys had once tried the trick but couldn't manage it. So had Oncle Édouard, but he had chewed up the whole candle and got a blister on his tongue and a pain in his stomach.

The explanation is a great secret, and if I let you in on it you must never tell another soul, or it won't be a secret any longer. The candle was really a piece of raw apple and the wick a very fresh almond. An oily almond burns easily, and if you are brave enough to put the 'candle' into your mouth, flame first and very quickly indeed, it goes out before it can hurt you. But you have to know exactly how to do it.

With that Christmas dinner ended and everyone went to the drawing room for the Christmas tree. And that was the end of a very long Christmas Day.

The Snow Fort and the Sugar Bush

IN WINTER THE OLD CITY OF QUEBEC ALWAYS had a great many snowstorms. The snow piled up in great banks along the streets and the trenches between the Glass Sea and the Citadel filled up with huge drifts. Even quite big children who jumped into these drifts could easily be buried up to their necks.

This particular year, the snowbanks opposite the family house being even higher than usual, Alain, Edmond, and Julie were inspired to make a fort during the Christmas holidays. They began by digging a deep hole at the top of a particularly big bank. Then they cut out blocks of snow elsewhere and with these built a wall around the fort. Julie worked inside the excavation while the rest busied themselves on the wall. By the time the holidays were over the wall was so high, and the hole so deep, that the younger

****

children could not have got down to the bottom of it if steps had not been cut into the snow.

On the afternoon of the day before school resumed for the older children a solemn ceremony was held, at which the fort was handed over to the younger ones. It ended with Julie running up a flag she had made and Alain and Edmond firing a royal salute of twenty-one guns with their toy pistols. They had plenty of ammunition for these firearms because Oncle Édouard had given them new boxes of caps for Christmas.

As, in spite of the steps, Tilly, Mic, Ethel, and Henri still found it hard to get through the top of the fort without help, they began to dig an entrance tunnel from the street. This was hard work, but at last it was finished and they could creep in on hands and knees. Beau-Charles gave them the top of an old wooden box to use as a door, so that now they were secure from attack. Then each one excavated a little private room. Jumbo worked with them and greatly enjoyed life inside a fortress.

The children worked so long and hard, and were so busy in their spare moments sliding down the Glass Sea, that they hardly noticed the sun getting warmer each day and the icicles beginning to melt. So they were taken by surprise one morning when

✢✢✢

Beau-Charles casually remarked, '*C'est du beau temps pour le sucre*' – it's fine weather for maple sugar. With a start they remembered that they always went to the sugar bush in Easter week.

Mother being out at the moment, they ran to Tante Mathilde who was sitting in the morning room knitting still more red leggings. They asked her when Easter was.

'Let me see,' she said. 'Alain and Edmond and Julie will be home next week on *Jeudi saint* – Maundy Thursday – so you'll probably go the following Monday or Tuesday. Which one of you will bring me back a little sugar house?'

In chorus they promised to bring Tante Mathilde her maple-sugar house. Then she told them a story. It was about some children who were walking in the forest when suddenly they found a sugar house big enough for them to set up housekeeping in. All the other children round about came to visit them. This story made them all the more anxious to go to the sugar bush. They even hoped they might meet the children who had found the big house and be invited to go in and see it.

On the Wednesday afternoon, the day before *Jeudi saint*, Alain and Edmond duly came home from boarding-school. To celebrate the homecoming the

whole family had tea together in the dining room
just as on Christmas Eve, and Rosalie made a cake
with maple icing on top and *Joyeux Pâques* – Happy
Easter – written on it. The children were terribly
excited when Father announced that the following
Tuesday was to be the great day.

   Easter Day and Easter Monday came and went
until at last it was Tuesday morning. The sky was a
clear blue and the sun shone warm and golden. In
the street, water trickled along the gutters and great
shining drops fell from the icicles on the eaves. Julie
couldn't find her moccasins because someone had
borrowed them and forgotten to put them back.
Henri hid Tilly's bloomers and when Mary Ann tried
to catch him to give him a 'bother' on the ear for
being naughty, he hid under his bed. Mary Ann
pushed the bed about but Henri crawled along with
it. At last she got a broom and swept him out. He

✢✢

got a few whacks on the behind, but they didn't hurt much because Mary Ann never smacked one very hard on the day of an outing.

At last everyone was ready to go. Beau-Charles carried the lunch hampers out to the sleighs. No less than three sleighs were standing by the door: their own with Narcisse on the box in his fur cap and gauntlets, and two belonging to Jerry McDermot and Narcisse's cousin Joe Lebeau. The children knew

these two men well because they always drove when there were too many to fit into the one family sleigh.

Because some of their cousins were also coming along, the first stop was in front of a house in the rue Saint-Louis. Here two more sleighs were waiting, with the uncle and aunt and some of the children in the first, and Nanou (whom we've already met in the park) and the rest of the children in the second.

The cabmen fastened the buffalo robes up round them, took the blankets off the horses, and got back up and cracked their whips. All five sleighs jingled merrily off with Narcisse in the lead.

Their destination was a sugar bush near Montmorency, the village at the top of the famous waterfall of that name that tumbles over the high cliff into the St Lawrence. If you visit Québec in summer you will be sure to drive out to this great sight, but if you come in winter you will see the huge ice cone that forms at the bottom of the falls from the freezing spray. Nowadays the trip doesn't take more than half an hour or so in a car, but in those days it took all morning by sleigh.

They arrived at lunch time, which is always a nice time to arrive anywhere. The sleighs drove straight through the village and then across a bridge before stopping in front of a big old house on the left-hand side of the road. This was a famous inn called Bureau's, where grown-ups went to toboggan parties – but of course the toboggan slide down the ice cone was much too dangerous for children.

Everyone was stiff and cold after the drive and very glad to get into the warm inn where a big wood fire blazed on the hearth and, best of all, to eat a hearty lunch. It began with steaming plates of pea soup, continued with veal-and-ham pie and cold turkey and heaps of sandwiches, and ended with crisp sugary *croquignoles* – doughnuts – fresh from the pot.

After lunch the innkeeper announced that three wood sleighs were waiting at the door to take them to the bush. Everyone put their heavy clothes back on and piled into the sleighs. You always stood up in wood sleighs because that way you could pack in more people.

The road was only a rough track across the brown fields. By this time of year the ground was bare except for white patches where snow lay in the hollows. The road was still frozen hard and stretched off into the distance in a dirty grey line. Crows sat on fence posts, cawing hoarsely as the sleighs approached. After a time the road dipped into a little valley and crossed a stream before winding deep into the woods. Here the ground became so soft that the horses had a hard time pulling the sleighs. Everyone got out and walked alongside to lighten the load – everyone, that is, but the ladies and nursemaids.

As they approached the camp the children ran ahead in great excitement.

'I'll be there first!' shouted Edmond.

'No, I will!' Julie and one of the cousins cried with one voice.

At that they all tried to run faster but soon found themselves floundering in a patch of wet snow. A dog barked somewhere in the woods, and then came a sound of chopping.

'We're getting close!' the children cried breathlessly to Father and Oncle Édouard behind them and raced ahead faster than ever. Soon the road took a sharp turn to the right and there, in a clearing just ahead, was the log *cabane à sucre* – the sugaring hut – with wisps of smoke curling up from its chimney. Two men were chopping wood and Monsieur Bédard, the owner of the hut, was just coming back from the woods. His big black dog Prince was pulling a little sledge on which rested a sap barrel that Monsieur Bédard steadied with his hand. The other men had just emptied another barrel into a big tub in the hut when they all caught sight of the visitors. Monsieur Bédard waved his cap vigorously.

'*Tiens, tiens, monsieur Joly*!' he shouted, leaving Prince and the sledge and running to meet them. '*Vous êtes bienvenus*!' – you are welcome. He shook them all by the hand and said what a fine year it was for maple sugar.

✦✦

'While I prepare *la tire*,' – the toffee – he continued, 'would you children like to go out for more sap?'

They wasted no time in setting out with Prince and Monsieur Bédard's nephew Alexandre, who was one of the woodcutters.

'*Tirez sur le nord*' – keep to the north – shouted Monsieur Bédard as they left. So they began emptying the sap buckets on that side of the road. They knew exactly which way to turn because, there being

no street signs in a maple wood, you learned to take directions from the sun.

Now I don't know whether you have ever been in a sugar bush, but in case you haven't I'll tell you what it is like. Each maple tree has a little hole bored into it fairly close to the ground. Just below this hole a little V-shaped gutter is driven in, to catch the sap as it drips out and direct it into a tin bucket hanging from the gutter. Sap runs best when there has been a hard frost the night before and there's warm sun during the day.

By the time the children returned, *la tire* was ready to commence. While they had been in the woods Monsieur Bédard and his men had made a snow table. To do this they had first gathered a heap of nice fresh snow and moulded it into a long narrow platform about a foot high and two feet wide. Then they pounded it down with their shovels to make it flat and smooth. Along its middle they laid a row of *palettes*, which are little wooden paddles like the ones you take to the seaside in summer, only smaller. They are all you need to eat the maple sugar.

When everyone was seated Monsieur Bédard and his nephew came out of the hut with an iron pot so big they had to carry it between them on a stick. On the snow at each place they poured out a big

✛✛

'pancake' of hot syrup. The way to eat this is to take your *palette* and fold in the edges of your sugar pancake and pop it into your month. When it is cold and with lots of snow sticking to it, nothing in the world can possibly taste better.

After they had all eaten more than enough, Monsieur Bédard and his men laid a collection of wooden moulds on the snow table. These sugar moulds are hollowed out in reverse into every shape you can think of: houses, animals, people, prayer-books, and many other things besides. Each mould is filled with hot syrup, left to cool, and then tapped out. Any syrup remaining in the pot is poured into little birch-bark *cassots* – cones – that look like hearts. Every child is given a *cassot* to take home.

'*C'est le coeur de votre cavalier*,' quipped Monsieur Bédard as he gave them to the girls, meaning that the cones were the sweet hearts of their sweet-hearts. That made everyone laugh, Monsieur Bédard more heartily than anyone else. Last of all the children chose a sugar house to take to Tante Mathilde and hearts for Beau-Charles, Yvonne, and Narcisse.

The flaming red sun was setting in the west as they drove back across the fields. Far over the St Lawrence the moon rose like a white ball in the clear green sky. Father and Oncle Édouard struck up the old French song Canadians love so well, '*Au clair de la lune*.' The drivers joined in and soon everyone was singing. As it grew darker, all that could be seen of the farmhouses along the way were their windows reflecting the sunset sky and their massive chimneys silhouetted against the last gleams in the west.

Far above, the stars came out one by one. Father pointed up to them. 'That's the Big Dipper,' he said, 'and one day I'll show you all the different pictures the stars make in the sky. But it's too late to start that tonight.'

The Log Drive

'HENRI,' SAID FATHER ONE SPRING MORNING at breakfast, 'how would you like to come along to the drive with Oncle Édouard and me today?'

'Oh really, really, may I?' he cried, jumping up and down in his chair in his excitement.

'Don't do that, Henri,' cautioned his mother, 'or you'll spill your milk!'

But he simply couldn't sit still, and you could hardly blame him because a log drive is one of the most thrilling things you can ever hope to see. Only people who own their own sawmills can ever go to one.

A log drive takes place early in spring when the logs that have been cut during the winter and stacked in the rollways along the banks of a river are floated down to the mill to be sawn into planks.

Father's sawmill was on the Seigneury, and every spring he went to be with his men on the drive. But besides being an exciting event it could be a dangerous one, especially when the logs jammed together in the river.

Ever since he could remember, Henri had longed for the day when he was old enough to go with Father. There are only a few years when you are just the right age, because you can't go when you are too little, or when you are bigger and have to be at school every day. Well, this year Henri was just old enough and just young enough. He could dress himself and remember to brush his teeth, but he hadn't yet started real school.

'Well, you can tell Mary Ann to pack your things,' said Father. 'She can use my old sack.'

When Henri found Mary Ann in the nursery she wasn't exactly overjoyed. 'You'll come back with a fine cold, my young larribuck,' she declared. But he didn't mind what he came back with just so long as he didn't come down with it before leaving. He didn't even mind her calling him a larribuck, for though it wasn't a very complimentary name, she never used it when she was really cross.

They were to leave just after lunch. Henri thought the morning would never end, but at last

✦✦✦

lunch was finished and it was time to go. He put on his blanket coat and fur cap, and Father and Oncle Édouard their short coats with red, black, and grey epaulets. Round their waists they all wore brightly coloured *ceintures fléchées* – Canadian arrow sashes – and on their feet *bottes sauvages* – Indian moccasins. While Mother stuffed things into the bags, Mary Ann slipped a brown-paper parcel into Henri's pocket.

'It's an orange and two *croquignoles* and two peppermints,' she said. 'You'll be hungry enough before you get there. Now mind, be a good boy and don't come back to me with dirty ears.' And then she kissed him as he went down to the sleighs. Narcisse fastened buffalo robes round them and picked up the reins. Henri waved good-bye to the family gathered at the window and felt very proud and happy.

In order to reach the railway station the sleighs had to cross the St Lawrence to Lévis. The ferry was a big, broad, paddle-wheel steamboat that looked for all the world like a fat white duck swimming in the water. Narcisse carried the bags and guns aboard and saw them into the public saloon of the ferry before he said good-bye and left.

The saloon was hot and crowded and smelled of so many things at once that you couldn't tell what they all were: not some good honest simple smell like onions or hair oil or *tabac canadien*. Three priests and quite a lot of nuns sat on the benches, the nuns in groups telling their beads or reading from their prayer-books. In one corner sat a lady whose five children were eating biscuits from a paper bag on her lap. Seeing them made Henri long to open Mary Ann's parcel, but he didn't like to do this when he was on a trip with grown-ups.

'I'm going outside for a breath of air,' said Oncle Édouard. 'It's too hot in here.'

The others followed him out on deck and found it even more crowded than the saloon. There were wood sleighs, one or two *carrioles* – passenger sleighs – and a two-horse sledge loaded with bags of flour. Boxes, bags, and barrels were piled everywhere. Two cows stood looking miserable, with bits of sacking over them, but the horses were happily feeding from their nosebags. Men stood about talking, smoking and spitting, most of them wearing shaggy fur coats, though some were dressed for the bush like Father and Oncle Édouard.

In a few moments the ferry whistled to signal its departure. The horses took fright and lunged about, while the cows seemed too unhappy to mind. The boat crunched its way through great sheets of ice, at times scarcely moving as the ice thumped against its sides and shook its timbers. When this happened the horses became excited again. One of them squealed and tried to bite its owner and only behaved when the man struck it with his whip. In the middle of the river the ice was less thickly packed and the boat got on more easily. Some of the ice had formed into great jagged islands separated by dark shiny patches of water.

As they drew near the opposite shore the ice became thick again and the boat's progress was slower. Men stood in the bow with coils of rope, ready to throw them to the wharf. The ferry now made crashing and roaring noises, and as the whistle blew the horses reared once more. Henri had to pretend he wasn't afraid. At last the wharf loomed before them like a wall of greenish-blue ice. The men at its edge caught the ropes and the ferry was safely tied up.

There was a great rush to debark. Loud sounds of shouting and the cracking of whips were heard as the sleighs bumped over the gangplank. A great many cabs were drawn up at the wharf, and as people got off the drivers sang out, 'Carriole, monsieur! carriole, madame!' Henri was secretly glad when Father took him by the hand.

Many of the passengers drove off at once, but the Jolys walked across the square to the railway station. They had some time to wait for the train, but Henri didn't mind because he was intently watching a big locomotive shunting about on the various tracks with a man on the cowcatcher. Suddenly there was a loud hoot and the train came puffing into sight round a shambles of sheds and houses. People poured from the station, all of them in a great hurry. Children cried, mothers scolded and dragged them along by the hand, and men scurried about with boxes and bags. When the train pulled up they jostled and scrambled to get aboard first.

The train seemed even more crowded than the ferry, but Henri and his father and uncle managed to find a double seat to settle into. Henri sat by the

✝✝

window and saw all that passed by: houses and shops and people, and then a lumberyard and a little frozen river across which the train rattled. After that there was open country where the fields were still under snow and little farmhouses and barns nestling under clumps of evergreens. Sometimes in the distance Henri could make out a church steeple and once or twice a sugar bush with its little huts.

They got out at a tiny station in the middle of the Seigneury woods. It was called a flag station, which meant that if you were waiting there and wanted the train to stop you had to wave a flag. Beside the track were a little platform, a house, and a shed. Beyond these was a deep gorge through which foamed a narrow river, with a trestle bridge over which the train would pass. Lights shone from the windows of the stationmaster's house, for the sun had set and the whole sky was aflame with red and gold.

Five or six men were waiting on the platform, and as the train came to a halt the door of the house opened and a woman appeared holding a tiny baby and sheltering four small children in her skirts. The men all shook hands with Father, patted his back and said, '*C'est de bon de vous revoir, Monsieur Joly*' – it's good to see you back. Then they loaded the bags and guns on their backs, and the party set out on a trail through the woods.

A good deal of snow lingered on the ground, and the trail was frozen hard except for a few muddy spots where the sun had penetrated. It was dark night when they reached the *chantier* – the logging hut – where a crowd of men came out to greet them. Henri felt very grown up to be met as if he too were a grown-up, but at the same time he felt just a little strange. He didn't actually wish he were at home, but he very nearly did.

Inside the hut they had a late supper of thick pea soup with salt pork, a rabbit stew with fried potatoes, apple pie with molasses, and tea. The men sat round smoking their pipes and telling Father how

the drive was going. A big fire roared in the stove and the air was blue with tobacco smoke and heavy with the smells of fried potatoes, coffee, onions, wet socks, and moccasins — and a great many other things as well.

After supper, as Father and Oncle Édouard filled their pipes, one of the men began playing the accordion. Father beat time on a tin plate. Two of the men leaped up and danced a jig while the rest clapped their hands and stamped their feet. After a short while Henri's eyes drooped and his head began to nod. For a moment he thought he was back on the ferry hearing the thud of the ice against the hull, but then his head jerked up and he realized it was only the music. The second time he woke it was to hear Father say, 'Well, well, I think it's time to turn in.' Henri felt proud to have stayed up so late.

The logging camp was at some distance from the *chantier*, which was on the bank of the same river that ran past the station. The night air was cold as Henri and his father and uncle stepped out of the warm hut. The moon shone brightly and all the stars were out. In the camp, the lamps were lit and a big fire roared in the stove. There were three rooms. In the first was a table, three old leather armchairs and the stove. The second had three bunks on either wall and a washstand and looking glass at its far end. The third room was the kitchen, and above it was a loft where the cook and his younger brother slept. All the bunks were filled with soft evergreen branches covered with red blankets. As Henri fell asleep in his bunk he thought he'd never slept in a more comfortable bed.

Next morning after an early breakfast he set off with Father and Oncle Édouard to watch the drive. For half a mile they tramped Indian file through the woods and came out on a high bank. Below them was the river, jammed solid with logs piled up in jagged heaps. Far upstream beyond the logjam was a stretch of open water, but downstream it was logs as far as the eye could see. Men were out working on the logs.

✛✛✛

'We'll have to dynamite them,' said the boss who was on the bank with Father.

'Yes, I'm afraid so,' replied Father.

Leaving Henri behind, Father and Oncle Édouard and the boss joined the men on the logs. To do this they had to climb and climb and jump a great deal. Four of the men then set out for the far bank and disappeared into the woods. When they emerged they were carrying a flatbottomed boat which they proceeded to set down on the logs. All the men except the boss and the boatman climbed back across the jam and up the bank where Henri stood.

Down on the river, the boss bent over something on the logs. Father put his hands to his mouth and shouted, 'Be careful!' and the boss waved and shouted back, '*Pas de danger*' – no danger. Henri saw him strike a match and then scramble away as fast as he could towards the man with the boat. The next moment there was a huge bang. The logs heaved up. Some were blown high into the air and great splinters were hurled up to the height of the trees. With a terrific roaring and cracking the whole jam began to move down river. The boss and his men jumped into the boat and were swept along with the jostling logs. They stood up, warding off the logs as best they could with their cant-hooks.

Suddenly Oncle Édouard called out, 'Xavier can't make it!' Henri saw that one of the men was out of the boat and standing on a little raft of tumbling logs. When this raft began to break apart he jumped to some other logs nearer to the boat, but these too parted and he was swept along on a single log, balancing himself with his hook.

Father, Oncle Édouard, and the other men on shore chased along the river bank to find a place from which they could go out to help Xavier. They soon disappeared among the trees, but Henri could still hear their shouts. He followed along as fast as he could go, to see what would happen. In a moment he caught sight of them. Off a little point of land they were up to their knees in the water, rescuing Xavier. When they got him safely to shore they lit a big fire and hung out their wet clothes and boots to dry. They made a big pot of coffee and sat round the fire drinking it and eating thick sandwiches of salt pork. Then they smoked their pipes before setting off to follow the drive down to another jam in the river.

It was dark before the Jolys returned to camp that evening. Birch logs crackled merrily in the stove and supper was ready. Henri sat with his father and uncle on the bunks, pulling off wet boots and putting on dry socks and slippers. They washed their hands in a tin basin and threw the water into the woods, then hung up the socks on a line and sat down at table. Henri ached all over with fatigue, but it was a lovely kind of tiredness and as soon as he finished his supper he fell fast asleep.

Each day there was something new to see. One morning as they walked through the woods they spotted some little red deer. Now when red deer are startled, all you can see of them are their white tails disappearing among the trees. At another time, deep in the woods, they came across a great hollow beaten down in the undergrowth as if with a spade. One of the men said, '*Encore un ravage*,' — *ravage* meaning a clearing trampled down by the deer, rather like a moose yard.

One evening on the way back from the drive they found the camp in a state of alarm. One old woodman had been badly injured by a falling log, and blood was spurting from a gash in his leg. When Father saw this he made a dash for his medicine chest. Oncle Édouard knelt beside the man, took out his handkerchief and wound it round the leg above the wound. This made the bleeding stop. Father came back and examined the injury. 'We shall have to wash your feet,' he told the man, 'or else you may become infected.' And he asked the cook to bring a kettle of hot water.

The old man took fright. 'Do you want to kill me, monsieur?' he cried. 'I haven't put my feet in hot water for forty years. The last time was the night before my wedding. If I do it now it will kill me for sure.'

Henri was shocked because he thought everybody in the world had a hot bath every Saturday evening. It took a great deal of persuading to get those feet into the water. The cook washed them while Father tied up the wound with clean bandages. Then the man was carried back to his bunk.

Too soon came the day to leave the camp. Henri had never in all his life been sorrier to go home than on that day. As they dressed, Oncle Édouard said, 'Better wash behind your ears, my boy. Mary Ann is sure to look there tonight.'

When they reached the station Father went off with one of his men to inspect some logs on the other side of the little river, while Oncle Édouard stayed behind with Henri talking to the stationmaster and his family.

It wasn't long before Father and the man began crossing the trestle bridge back to the station. Suddenly, while they were on the middle of the bridge, a loud whistle blew and the train came roaring out of a deep cutting on the far bank. Father and the man hurriedly glanced over their shoulders, stepped over the rails, and threw themselves face down on the narrow ledge between the track and the raging torrent below. Oncle Édouard cried out as the stationmaster waved his flag furiously and his wife threw up her hands and screamed. The train thundered over the bridge and came to a screeching halt on the other side of the station. The engine driver and the fireman leaped down and raced back to the station as the passengers poured out of the carriages. Oncle Édouard and the stationmaster rushed to the bridge with the others hard on their heels.

Henri couldn't help crying, but fortunately nobody noticed. Then he saw his father standing up on the bridge. He pushed his way through the crowd until he found Father and threw his arms round him.

'*Le bon Dieu nous a sauvés, mes amis*' – the good Lord has saved us – said Father to the crowd. 'We shall have a mass said in thanksgiving for our deliverance.'

Everyone returned to the station. The stationmaster ran into his house and brought out a square black bottle from which he gave Father a drink before the train left for Quebec.

'Don't say anything to your mother about this,' said Father when they were settled into their seats. Henri promised he wouldn't and he never did.

Off to the Seigneury

ONCE SPRING REALLY GETS STARTED IN Quebec, it proceeds with a vengeance. One day there are snowbanks lining the streets and icicles hanging from the eaves; the very next day the icicles are gone and the snow has turned to slush. Before you know it the grass has become green and dandelions are springing up. It's then that you begin thinking of summer holidays in the country.

Tilly, Mic, Ethel, and Henri came home from school the first day after the Easter holidays to find streams of grey water rushing along the gutters. In Quebec, as you know, all the streets are hills and in spring they become mountain streams. They are ideal for making dams.

This particular spring the children made a splendid dam at the corner of their street where it turned downhill. After a little lake had formed, they opened the dam. The water gushed out and poured down the street, and they ran alongside it clearing a channel with their spades. They had to be quick about it because at any moment the channel might be blocked and spill over on the pavement. Then somebody's cook was sure to come out of a house and threaten to 'tell their pa and ma' that they were flooding her kitchen. Next to having their doorbells rung by naughty children, nothing made cooks so angry as dams.

Very soon the long slope of the Glass Sea lay bare and brown. One afternoon while the children were playing there, some big boys set the dry grass afire. Year after year this happened; no one ever knew exactly who did it, but once a fire started everyone joined in to beat it out. And so on this April afternoon groups of children appeared from nowhere armed with sticks. The Jolys were among them, revelling in the excitement and pretending they were early settlers caught in a forest fire.

But soon it became a little too much like a real forest fire for comfort. Flames licked through the grass, leaving behind them swaths of blackened earth and clouds of smoke. It was great fun to run alongside the fire trying to beat it out, your eyes smarting from the smoke. But today a strong wind sent the

✠✠✠

flames crackling through the grass more quickly than anyone could keep up with them. When one boy shouted, 'The police'll come!' the crowd disappeared as if by magic. The next moment maids in their caps and aprons ran out of the houses with pails of water. Narcisse and Beau-Charles and all the neighbourhood menservants came too. All along the street people hung out of windows to see what was going on.

Mary Ann was one of them. She darted out and dragged the Joly children back to the pavement. She had hardly got them all together when there arose a great clatter and the rapid ding, ding, ding of a bell came closer and closer. With a flourish two

✦✦

big horses dashed round the corner pulling a red fire engine with firemen in shining helmets on the running boards. These men quickly disposed of the fire, climbed back on the engines, and drove away.

The children were only too glad to go home with Mary Ann because, with the front door shut behind them, no policeman could come in unless Beau-Charles let him in. The danger was past, but Mary Ann roundly scolded them for getting mixed up with 'a pack of dirty ruffians.' She ended with a long lecture on how Christian children of good family ought to behave.

It was not long, however, before the blackened slope turned green, because once old grass is burned away the new has a better chance to grow. It was only a matter of time now before the younger children would go to the country. Soon Beau-Charles and Narcisse were carrying down the big basket trunks from the attics, and Yvonne and Philomène were going round with a stepladder, taking down curtains and spreading dust sheets over the furniture. In the nursery Mary Ann busied herself all day long with packing. So busy indeed was the whole house that the children were left to do pretty much as they liked.

That was how it happened that two days before they were to leave Henri disgraced himself. It was such a warm day that all the children were sent out to play. Usually Mary Ann went with them, but this morning they started off alone. When they passed the upper landing, and the nursery door had shut behind them, Henri's high spirits got the better of him and he climbed on the banister – which was something he was strictly forbidden to do in case he lost his balance and fell off at the place where the banister curved sharply down to the ground floor. You could even fall straight down to the entrance hall and on to the coal stove at the foot of the stairs.

Well, just as Henri embarked on the banister the nursery door opened and he saw Mary Ann with an armful of clothes. He was so startled that he lost his grip and went hurtling down at top speed. Luckily for him Mother was at the landing talking to Tante Mathilde and caught him just as he lost his balance. Mary Ann let out a whoop, dropped the clothes, and rushed down. Beau-Charles came panting up the stairs and between them they hauled Henri off the banister and set him down.

Relieved and thankful as Mother was, she nevertheless took Henri to her room for a spanking.

✣✣

The other children sat on the stairs feeling sorry for him as they heard the smack of Mother's slipper and Henri bawling out, 'I'll be good, mamma, I'll be good! Not with the heel, mamma!' Of course she never spanked him with the heel, but when you are being spanked it feels as if a slipper is all heel.

At last came the day for the parents and the younger children to leave for Platon, the three elder children being still in boarding school. The trunks were strapped up, the tea baskets were packed, and Jumbo was on his leash. Lunch was early because the ship was due to sail at two o'clock. By the time they had finished the soup, cold meat, and bread and butter which made lunch seem more like a picnic, Mary Ann, Yvonne, and Philomène were frantically stuffing in all the forgotten items and the men were carrying the luggage to an express wagon outside. Then the family packed themselves into the rockaway, said good-bye to their friends gathered on the pavement, and were off. The children waved back as they drove down the street, feeling a little superior to be going to the country earlier than any of their friends.

The wharf in Lower Town was crowded because this was a Saturday and the farmers were going home after Friday market, and taking home all the things they hadn't sold. There were boxes of squealing pigs, wicker cages of hens, two cows, a number of calves, and a few sheep. Amid these and all the luggage the people jostled one another, talked and laughed and smoked. Mother and Mary Ann led the way through the crowds and on to the ship.

Father met them at the gangway. He led them to the upper deck and into the public saloon which was full of people sleeping or just sitting and talking. At the far end was a door marked in large letters

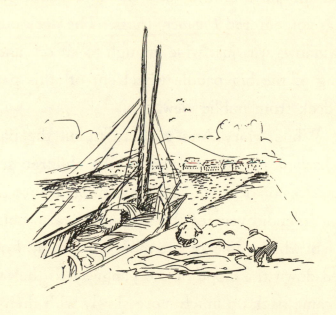

Première Classe. Father opened this door and the family went in. The first class saloon was much grander than the public one, and the children felt very grand to be in it. In the middle of its oilcloth-covered floor stood a round table with a red cloth, and on each side of it was a big rocking chair. Two nuns sat there reading their prayer-books. Near the door a little girl in a black convent dress was playing 'Home, Sweet Home' on the harmonium. On either side of the room were the doors of the private cabins, and at the far end was a curving bench that followed the contours of the stern, with a door in its middle opening on to a narrow deck.

The Jolys always took the first cabin on the left as you entered *Première Classe*. The deck outside its windows was just wide enough to sit on, and the casing of the big paddle wheel cut off this part of the deck from public view.

While Mary Ann tried to fit all the parcels and baskets into the tiny cabin, the children settled themselves on deck to see what went on ashore. They had a splendid view of the loading of farm animals, some of which came aboard most unwillingly. Porters raced down the slope of the gangway to the wharf, but came back up much more slowly with their barrows piled high with luggage.

Finally the ropes were untied from the wharf, the paddle wheels began to turn, and the ship pulled out into the river. It usually took the *Sainte-Marie* – for such was her name – about three hours to reach Pointe-Platon, but no one could ever predict exactly how long it would be, not even the captain. If asked, he would shrug his shoulders, throw up his hands and say, '*Ah ça, monsieur, ça dépend du bon Dieu, et du vent, et de la mer et de la charge*' – that depends on the good Lord, the wind, the tide, and the load. But he was seldom asked because nobody really cared how long the journey took: the longer the better because it offered such a wonderful opportunity to see one's friends and catch up on all the news.

And so the *Sainte-Marie* lazily wound her way back and forth from one shore to the other, stopping at one village after another. As she approached each stop she churned the water furiously and blew her whistle to announce her arrival. Men on the wharf shouted up to the crew, people got off, a great deal of cargo was unloaded, and the landing stage was crowded with carts to take the people home. The passengers staying aboard came out on deck hoping to catch a glimpse of some relative or friend on shore. After the people, it was the animals' turn to disembark. Cows refused to walk the gang-plank until

✠✠

their owners twisted their tails. Sheep had to be pushed from behind, as their tails were too short to twist; or else the men caught them by their wool and hauled them off bleating to the wharf.

By four o'clock it was tea time on board, a meal to which the children had been looking forward ever since morning. On their own little deck two stools were put together to make a table. Inside the cabin Mary Ann made tea and handed the baskets through the window while Mother and Oncle

Édouard laid the table. As a special treat there was lemonade instead of milk to drink, and sandwiches and cakes and bananas — and no knives and forks and spoons to bother with.

Shortly after tea was finished and the plates and mugs were put away, the village of Cap-Santé came into sight. It lies on the north shore just across the St Lawrence from Pointe-Platon. Soon the children could make out the two tall spires of the village church and, on a road leading to the landing stage, a man in a cart galloping down as if he thought the ship might leave before he got there.

The departure from Cap-Santé was the signal for Mary Ann to take the children to the cabin to tidy them up before landing. She brushed their hair and wiped their faces with the corner of a damp towel – oh, how they hated this! – then put on their coats and hats and sent them to wait on deck with Mother.

And then at last they were on their way across the river. In their excitement they could hardly sit still; and that was because the pleasure of landing was always spiced with a sense of danger. Anything might happen. They might be separated from Mary Ann and get lost amid the freight; the *Sainte-Marie* might leave before they got off; or they might fall beneath a horse or be carried away in a flock of panicking sheep – as once happened to Julie.

But the engines had hardly stopped when the cabin door opened and there stood Napoléon, Father's head man at Platon, accompanied by his nephew Joe. These two were great friends of the children and after shaking hands all round they gathered up

✠✠✠

the luggage. The great moment was at hand. Father took Mother's arm, Oncle Édouard took Tante Mathilde's and Mary Ann took Ethel's and Henri's hands. Napoléon and Joe made a way through the crowd for the little procession. The tide was out and the wharf towered above the ship like a high wall with bits of green seaweed clinging to it. The gangway made such a steep ascent that it took two sailors to help Mary Ann and the children up.

Narcisse and his summer helper Cléophas were waiting on the slip with the carriages, their horses dancing nervously at being so near the water. As they started off they tossed their manes and Narcisse had to wind the reins tightly round his wrists and shout, '*Arrié, arrié donc!*' – slow down.

It was only a short drive up the hill. The narrow road led past Narcisse's house and along a straight stretch across fields that lay beneath a steep wooded bank. Then it divided in a V with one part leading straight ahead and the other through a low white gate. The carriages sped through this gate and climbed to the top where stood a lone elm on the one side and the garden hedge on the other. Finally the road took a sharp turn left round a clump of trees – and there stood Platon manor house.

It was a high two-storeyed building designed like a large version of a Swiss chalet. White wooden

verandas with a pattern of maple-leaves cut into their lattice-work ran round both storeys. These and the walls were covered with Virginia creeper. The door was wide open and Madame Napoléon stood on the steps to welcome the family.

If a house is one's own, there are things about it that make it different from any other in the world. It has a special smell and a special creak of the floors when you walk on them. It has dark spooky corners and marks on the walls which have their own stories to tell. Such a house was Platon. There was the cloak-room which you had to pass so often, and which frightened you each time because you remembered that it was pitch-black inside and the shadowy clothes hanging on hooks reminded you of the bodies suspended on the walls of Bluebeard's chamber. Then there was that one spindle on the stair that was a paler brown than the others. It was a new one because

✠✠

once when Mary Ann was taking Alain upstairs he kicked her shins and she smacked him; and between them they broke it.

Supper was nearly ready, and as soon as Madame Napoléon had kissed the children and told them how much they had grown, they raced up to the nursery to wash and brush up. It was such an event to have supper in the dining room with the grown-ups that they willingly submitted to Mary Ann's efforts to make them neat and clean and didn't even squirm when she brushed their hair.

During the meal they heard the hay cart arriving with the luggage. They longed to go out of doors and see their rabbits, their swing, and their own little Bird's Nest Cottage. But it was already dark when supper was finished, and Mary Ann took them straight up to bed. As she led the way they looked out and saw the lighted lanterns on the carriages and that made them feel it was very late to be up.

Soon they were safely tucked up in their *baudets* – their trestle beds. Mary Ann finished putting their things away in drawers and then turned down the oil lamp on the nursery table. As they snuggled under the warm bed-clothes they thought of all the nice things they were going to do at Platon. When you first arrive it seems as if summer will last for ever.

On the Beach

IT WAS NOT LONG BEFORE JULIE, EDMOND, and Alain finished school in Quebec and joined the younger children at Platon. The family was now reunited and could settle down to enjoy the holidays. The older children had hardly been there a week when one morning Oncle Édouard proposed a minnowing expedition. The purpose of this was to catch a good supply of bait for fishing for bass and *doré* – walleye – off the wharf. I don't know whether you have ever been out catching minnows, but if you have you'll know what hard work it is.

All the children went off with their uncle that very morning. Down at the beach they took off their shoes and stockings. The girls tucked up their skirts as high as they could – in those days no one wore shorts – and the boys rolled up their trouser legs above their kness.

✦✦

The tide always went very far out at Platon and exposed a broad expanse of sand dotted with shallow reedy pools that were full of tiny grey minnows. Oncle Édouard and Alain carried a big sheet between them, and Julie and Edmond a wooden bucket slung on a pole. The younger children had small hand-nets and tin buckets. When they came to a pool containing a shoal of minnows, Alain and his uncle held opposite ends of the sheet. Bending down, they placed one end of the sheet just above the water and the other end near the bottom of the pool. Then they made a great scoop and the entire shoal was swept up into the dry part of the sheet. From it Julie and Edmond bailed the minnows out into the bucket.

Meanwhile the other children ran about finding smaller pools and netting the minnows in them. Sometimes they went over the bigger pools a second time, picking up the stragglers that darted in and out among the reeds. But when the younger children's legs began to ache they wandered back along the beach looking for a good place to build a campfire.

They were very fond of campfires, but on this particular occasion their thoughts were interrupted when Mic shouted suddenly and waved from a distance along the beach. They all raced to the little point on which she stood, and there, to their great surprise, half-hidden in the tall reeds, was an old-fashioned flat-bottomed boat. They examined her to see whether she had a name but none was to be found.

'I suppose all the people in her were drowned,' said Henri, 'so we can keep her.'

'We'll have to tell everybody about finding her, and have her *crié* in church,' said Tilly. 'The people's relatives may want her back.' In those days, you see, when anyone in a country parish lost or found any-thing it would be called out in church rather than being advertised in the newspaper as one did in town. At the end of Sunday mass, the *bédeau* – the sexton

– would go up into a little square box at the front of the church and read out all the things that had been lost or found, and in that way most things got back to their rightful owners.

Oncle Édouard and the older boys had also heard Mic calling and they too came running. Alain and Edmond were especially excited because they had always longed to have a boat of their own. They duly examined the hulk for holes but declared her sound though very dirty. Worst of all, she smelled of everything bad you could think of rolled into one.

'We'll have to give her a good cleaning and a coat of paint and put a mast in her,' declared Alain. 'And then we can sail her up and down the whole of our shoreline.'

'But first we'll have to christen her,' said Julie who was very religious.

'I should just call her the *Rancid Butter*,' suggested Oncle Édouard, 'because you can smell her a mile away.'

Tilly and Mic didn't much like this idea, and of course Julie thought she should be named after a saint. But the boys approved the name and decided she should have a proper launching once she was done up. They pulled her above high-water mark to keep her safe until they could come back for her with a hay cart. All the way home they talked of nothing but the wonderful trips they would take in her.

Mary Ann was anything but pleased when she heard of the discovery. 'I've a mind to go and burn the dratted thing before you start off getting yourselves drowned!' she declared. But then Mary Ann never liked new ideas.

That same afternoon the children and their uncle, with Cléophas to help, went back to the beach and hauled the *Rancid Butter* off in a cart to the *boutique* – the workshop – where her cleaning began. Father and Mother came down to look. They thought she would make a fine boat but agreed that the name was fitting. Madame Joly held her nose all the time they were inspecting the boat.

The children worked hard all that week. They scraped off the dirt and scrubbed and caulked their craft, and last of all Cléophas made her a mast. Father presented them with a big pot of red paint so that she became red all over except for a yellow band running round her and her name, which Oncle Édouard painted on her sides in big yellow letters. When she was finished, no one would have recognized her but for the smell. No amount of 'Lifebuoy' soap could ever have got rid of that. It was as much a part of her as her very shape.

✦✦✦

On the day of the launching there was to be a picnic supper on the beach. But before that took place Mother officially christened the boat with a bottle of raspberry vinegar mixed with water, looking exactly like wine. Then the elders went out for the first spin. Though they had to row because there wasn't wind enough to fill the sail, they hoisted it just the same. For, as Oncle Édouard said, it made her look like a seasoned veteran of the seas. The children liked that because it made them think the *Rancid Butter* might really have been a pirate brig flying the blackjack which had seen all sorts of adventures on the high seas before drifting to Platon.

As soon as the first boatload returned, a second went out with Father, for it was a part of the ceremonies that everyone should have a trip. Mary Ann threatened to be the only exception, declaring, 'I don't hold with the sea when there's the Lord's and the Blessed Virgin's good earth to stand on.' But she finally let herself be persuaded and sat uneasily in the stern clutching her petticoats about her. 'Don't go far, now!' she cried. 'And none of your tricks!' She didn't pretend to be sorry when the keel grated on the beach and the boys leaped out to help her to shore.

'The very first time one of you is drowned in this craft,' she declared, 'I'll see she's destroyed.'

It was a different matter with Tante Mathilde, who in spite of her blindness loved every moment of her trip. '*Que c'est donc beau d'être sur la mer!*' – how lovely to be on the sea – she exclaimed, and began singing the old French song '*Il était un petit navire.*' She was game for anything.

After everyone had been out it was time for supper. A big fire had been lit on the beach and tall stacks of buttered toast lay beside it. Julie and Mary Ann stirred the frying-pans and soon everyone was sitting round the fire with plates of scrambled eggs and toast and mugs of tea. After that came more toast and strawberry jam. When the dishes were washed and dried and the baskets packed up, the children gathered armfuls of driftwood and rebuilt the fire. As it blazed merrily they sat in a circle and

✦✦✦

sang songs like '*Au clair de la lune*,' 'Way down upon the Swannee River,' '*Alouette*' and '*Frère Jacques*.'

As they sang, the tide came lapping in until it came within a few feet of the fire. The setting sun made a great sweep of gold on the river as it slowly sank over the far shore. The sky turned scarlet, and then a clear green which faded into black. The stars came out and a full moon rose. Beyond the magic circle on the beach all was lost in shadow.

After the singing Oncle Édouard began to tell bloodcurdling stories from India, of lions and tigers and of terrible battles with wild tribesmen, until shivers ran up and down the children's spines. Just at that moment a sound of wheels and hoofs came out of the darkness. Everyone was startled and waited breathlessly for a band of hill warriors to spring out and surround them. But the dying fire revealed only the faces of Narcisse and Cléophas who had come to take them home. The children scrambled to their feet and, keeping close to the grown-ups, stumbled through the darkness to the carriages.

The *Rancid Butter*, which no owner ever claimed, kept them busy for the next few weeks. Father made it a rule that no one could go out in her who couldn't swim twenty yards. So she was anchored near the bath-house and competitions were held for falling overboard and swimming to shore, and drills for rescuing anyone in trouble.

A hot dispute arose over who was to be captain. Mic claimed the honour as it was she who had found the boat. The boys didn't like the idea of a girl captain; but at the same time they were afraid of Mic's temper, for when she flew into a rage there was nothing she wouldn't do. On this occasion she climbed up the wharf and threatened to jump off. The others knew she would be drowned; and besides, Mary Ann would be furious with all of them. Oncle Édouard settled the argument by appointing Mic captain and Edmond admiral. An admiral is certainly higher up than a captain, but the captain is in charge of his ship; yet Mic would have to obey the admiral or else be court-martialed and lose her command. It was a neat balance of authority and it worked well.

The Sawmill

THE CHILDREN WERE SO ABSORBED IN THE
boat that they very nearly forgot what they had always
thought to be the best treat of the whole summer.
It was Father who reminded them of it. At breakfast
one morning he announced, 'I'm going to Sainte-
Émélie today with your mother and Oncle Édouard.
Julie and Mic, would you like to come along?' The
two girls were thrilled. Once a week Father drove
out to his saw mill on the Rivière du Chêne to talk
to his agent, and he always took one or two of the
children with him. But, to tell the truth, it had been
Oncle Édouard's idea to take Mic on this occasion,
because he has afraid of a mutiny breaking out against
the captain of the *Rancid Butter* while he was away.

The little village of Sainte-Émélie was twelve
miles from Platon. That meant a carriage drive that

＊✦＊✦＊✦＊✦＊✦＊✦＊✦＊✦＊✦＊✦＊✦＊✦＊✦＊✦＊✦＊

took all morning, but the girls knew they would love every minute of it. The road ran along the high bank of the St Lawrence. At the half-way point it passed the handsome parish church of the village of Lotbinière, with its two tall spires. One of the former maids at Platon had married the village baker, and the family would sometimes drop in on her. The children loved that, because she would always let them take several of her delicious little pink cakes from a glass dish on her sideboard. They probably stopped there this particular morning, but I don't know for sure.

At any rate, promptly on the stroke of ten the two best carriages drew up at the door of the manor house. Monsieur Joly liked to be punctual: '*L'exactitude est la politesse des rois,*' he would say, quoting the famous saying of King Louis XVIII. Father, Julie, and Mic boarded the first carriage and Mother and Oncle Édouard, the second. The grown-ups were in their best clothes: Father in a white suit made from the wool of his own sheep, Mother in a white dress with a black belt and a wide straw hat trimmed with black lace, and Oncle Édouard in the pongee suit and pith helmet he wore in India.

The horses trotted sedately along the sunflecked avenue and out through the gates into the

✦✦✦

highroad. Here they turned right and climbed a long hill leading to the highest level of Pointe-Platon. The horses stopped to rest half-way up, but once at the top they cantered briskly down the other side. It was a perfect summer day with a soft blue sky strewn with puffy white clouds. The fields were enamelled with buttercups and daisies, and the river stretched out far below in a gleaming blue sheet. The air was so clear that the children could see the little white dots of farmhouses on the opposite shore and even the spires of Cap-Santé church. All along the way people were gardening, spreading out washing to dry, drawing water from wells, or shoving trays of bread into outdoor ovens. Now and then the carriages would pass hay carts with children perched on the very top of their loads. The carts courteously pulled to one side to let them pass, and Father waved his thanks. The whole world basked happily in the sunshine.

On the way Father told a story. He was a very good story-teller and even Julie, who was all of thirteen, thrilled to his tale of a man who had a million-dollar bank-note and had the most terrible time trying to spend it. Nobody could make change for him wherever he went. So enthralled were both girls that they were astonished to see the tall elms and neat houses of Sainte-Émélie appear so soon.

In a moment the carriages clattered over a bridge and drew up in front of the agent's grey-and-white cottage.

The agent, Monsieur Parrot, was waiting at the gate. The cottage door opened and his wife bustled down the steps to join him. She was a thin, neat woman whose smooth black hair was brushed back into a tight bun at the back of her head. Over her black dress she wore a snowy apron trimmed with lace. After they had all shaken hands she took Mother and the girls upstairs to tidy up before lunch. Then she left them in the *salon* where Father, Oncle Édouard, and Monsieur Parrot were already talking business. In a few moments she returned to announce lunch.

Her lunches were always delicious. Father called her a *cordon bleu*, meaning that she was a blue-ribbon cook. That day she gave them a wonderful *soupe au chou* – cabbage soup – followed by roast pork with golden-brown potatoes, and there were fried eggs and bacon as well. Her dessert was white of egg beaten up with applesauce. Last of all came wild strawberry preserve with thick cream and slices of her *tarte à Lafayette* – a layer cake with thick white icing – and great dishes of *sucre à la crème* – a fudge-like maple sweet. When they had finished all this they could hardly move. The men went out on the

gallery to smoke their pipes while the others chatted in the *salon*. The Parrots' eldest daughter Marie-Louise, who had been married the previous autumn, brought in her new baby for Madame Joly to see, and she allowed the two girls to hold it in turn.

When the men had finished their pipes, the whole family set out for the mill, which was only a ten-minute walk from the cottage. As they came near it they were greeted by the wonderful smell of fresh-cut wood and damp bark. By the side of the road yellow planks were stacked in neat piles ready to be shipped to Quebec. At the mill itself there was a great bustle as empty carts rolled up to be loaded and the drivers shouted to the horses. Father and

Monsieur Parrot led the family past the mill to a dam on the Rivière du Chêne, stopping to chat with all the men they met on the way.

The river above the dam was full of logs. Two men stood one on either side of the big sluice – the mill race – through which the logs had to pass on their way to the race that took them into the mill. With their cant-hooks they saw to it that each log floated along freely. But sometimes a jam developed, and they had to go out over the logs to break it up. When they saw Father they stopped working and called out, '*Bonjour, monsieur, c'est bon de vous revoir*' – it's good to see you again. The man closest to Father came up on the bank. Because his hands were so dirty he spat liberally on them and wiped them on his trousers before shaking hands.

Then the family went inside the mill. First they watched the logs clattering in from the race in endless succession. They they went to see the sawing, which was the most exciting part of the mill. It was so noisy that they had to shout to one another. Huge saws either whirled round or jumped up and down, making a loud 'sh-shzz' sound as they cut the logs into planks. The floor was deep in sawdust and bark and trimmings from the logs, and the whole place smelled of fresh wood, oil, and tobacco smoke.

Julie and Mic didn't much like the sharp-toothed saws and their restless motion. The men attending the machines were as placid as if they were in the quiet of their own homes, but the girls gathered their skirts round them because Mother had told them a horrifying story of a friend who had gone to see her husband's mill just after she was married. Her skirt had got caught in the machinery and she was dragged in and killed. Then there was Narcisse's cousin Jean-Baptiste Lemay whose arm was cut off by a saw. So they were glad enough to leave the mill.

Back outside, Monsieur Parrot asked whether they would like to see a new colt, and of course they eagerly followed him up the river road. In a little field shaded by two elms a shaggy black mare grazed beside the fence. At her side was a long-legged jet-black colt with a white patch on his forehead and a soft pink nose.

'*C'est Fanny*,' said Monsieur Parrot pointing to the mare. 'She's one of the best *chantier* horses.'

'I remember her, of course,' said Father. 'She was born at Platon, and that's a fine little foal she has.'

'*C'est un vrai petit malin*' – he's a regular little rascal – said the agent with a laugh.

Just then, as if he understood what was said about him, the foal began to caper about and then ran back to his mother to make sure she was still there.

'He will make a fine strong draught horse,' said Father as they turned back towards the village.

'Unless I'm mistaken,' replied Monsieur Parrot, 'he isn't suited to that. He'd do better at Platon as a carriage horse. *C'est un cheval de race, ce petit-là*' – he's a thoroughbred, that little fellow.

'Oh, do let him come to us!' begged Julie and Mic in unison.

'We shall see about that when he growns up,' Father replied. 'It will be a long time before he is old enough to leave his mother.'

As they walked along, Father asked the girls if they would like to see the boats being loaded. It was a pretty long walk to the mouth of the little river in the heat of the day, but the road was shaded by tall trees on either side. The river banks were reinforced with wooden retaining walls, so that the water was as smooth and dark as in a canal. Two or three loaded carts passed them on the road, and several empty ones rattled back to the mill.

When they reached the point where the Rivière du Chêne emptied into the St Lawrence, they saw three *bateaux* being loaded. *Bateaux* are long low boats with tall masts and square sails, which carry

✛✛

heavy loads of freight up and down the great river.
When you see one at a distance it looks like a little
island of timber or hay drifting along the river.

Nearly as much went on here as at the mill.
Planks were stacked everywhere and men unloaded
still more from the carts. One of the *bateau* captains
who evidently oversaw the whole operation came over
to greet the family. Though he was in shirt-sleeves
the girls knew at once he was a captain from his cap
trimmed with gold braid. While Father and Oncle
Édouard went off with him to see how the work was
going, Mother and the girls sat in the shade. They
got very hot as they waited and were greatly relieved
when the men finally returned. The captain was mop-
ping his brow and Oncle Édouard had taken off his
topee. 'Worse than India,' he declared as the family
thankfully headed back to the Parrots' cottage.

A day at the old mill always ended with a game
of croquet with the Parrot children. Today the seven
youngest of these were waiting at the cottage. Croquet was a very popular game in those days and every
house of any importance had a neat little green – as
well as a *balançoire* where you could sit and swing
all afternoon. The Parrots' lawn lay beside the road,
with a picket fence and a row of elms to screen it,
and a bench for spectators. Their croquet set was

kept as freshly painted as everything else about the house. The mallets had short handles, and it wasn't against the rules to hold them down near the head or take a shot from between your legs, because the more you croqueted your opponent's ball the better. Those not playing ran around advising the players how to hit the ball, so that everyone took an active part in the game.

Mic had just hit the post and won the game when the men came through the gate. This meant the visit was over and it was time to go home. As the carriages drove up to the gate, Julie and Mic ran upstairs for their hats and the whole Parrot family gathered to say good-bye. There were many *au revoirs* and wavings of hands before the Jolys were out of sight and sound.

It grew dark on the way home. Lights were lit in the cottages along the road, and through their

open doors you could see families in their kitchens
saying the evening rosary. As the carriages came
close to the lighthouse at Pointe-Platon the big lamp
was already sweeping the dark fields with its great
beam. The children always had that spooky 'look-
behind-you' feeling whenever they passed the lighthouse, because Yvonne had told them of the Sunday
party there long ago that her old grandmother had
gone to. The devil had suddenly appeared through
a flaming hole in the floor and snatched the lighthouse
keeper's mother-in-law into it. It turned out that she
had secretly murdered her son-in-law and a poor

✛✛

Syrian peddler who had spent the night in the light-house had been wrongfully hanged for the crime. So in the end the wicked old woman had got her just deserts.*

It was blackest night when the travellers finally arrived home. The rest of the family were waiting on the veranda and Narcisse and Cléophas came running to take the horses to the stable. The girls felt stiff and cramped after the long drive but very happy to have had such a wonderful outing.

---

* cf. 'The Lighthouse of Ste. Julie' in Hazel Boswell's *Legends of Quebec* (Toronto and Montreal: McClelland and Stewart 1966), pp. 49-60.

The Raft

SUMMER, WITH ITS LONG DAYS OF GOLDEN
sunshine and deep blue skies, gradually ran its course.
Strawberries ripened and then raspberries and last
of all apples. By September the orchard was richly
hung with big red 'St Lawrence' and *Fameuse* apples
and yellow crab apples. Each morning in the tall
grass beneath the trees there were half a dozen windfalls, dewy and cool and sometimes with fat slugs
crawling over them. In the kitchen garden sweet corn
matured. After breakfast Mother and old *père* Beaudet the gardener walked up and down the rows pulling
at the green husks to see which ears were ripe.

The weeks when late summer merged into
autumn were a time of wonderful expeditions. Every
day Father and Oncle Édouard, Edmond and Alain,
and any others who were staying at Platon would go

✳✳

shooting snipe or partridge or duck. The rest of the family would join them for a picnic tea at some agreed-upon place.

And so at half-past three on any clear warm day Mother and the younger children would set out with picnic baskets and tea-kettle and drive along the beach or into the woods to the rendezvous. When they arrived and the horses were tied up and the carriages unloaded, preparations for tea began. The children would run off to gather firewood. Mother and the other grown-ups would spread out rugs, unpack the baskets, and slice the bread for toast. Tante Mathilde would make toasting forks with Henri to help her, he cutting five or six long twigs and smoothing them off, and she sharpening them. By the time the men returned a fire would be blazing and tea would be ready.

Afterwards, when evening came, they all sat round the fire singing old songs and telling stories. In the circle of yellow light they were warm and cosy, but when the time came to stamp out the fire and leave for home the air was cold. As they made their way in the dark to the carriages they walked Indian file, each holding on to the one ahead. The horses, restless after their long wait, flew along the road, snorting as they passed through the patches of white

✦✦✦

moonlight or when small animals scuttled across their path. It was pitch black when they turned into the gates, but ahead the windows of Platon shone with amber light. Beyond the dark mass of the house stretched the broad moonlit river.

One night on the way home Father said, 'We are in for a change in the weather. The glass has been falling, and just look at the moon.' The children looked, and sure enough it had a misty ring round it. The wind soughed in the trees, making them think of all the ghost stories they had ever heard. Julie whispered, 'All good spirits fear the Lord,' which is a sort of magic spell against ghosts.

Narcisse and Cléophas were waiting at the steps with lanterns. 'You've got back just in time,' said Narcisse. 'We're in for a storm tonight!'

He was right. Soon the wind came whistling round the house, then a crack of thunder and a dash of rain that sounded like pebbles thrown at the windows. It was lovely to lie in bed and hear the wind howling, the rain beating upon the roof, and the thunder crashing round the house. Under her warm bedclothes Julie began to pray for the poor souls caught in the storm, but she fell asleep before she could finish her prayer.

Next morning before prayers Alain dashed downstairs bursting with excitement. 'There's a huge raft down at the wharf,' he cried, 'the biggest that's ever been here!' The rest of the children caught the infection and raced out to the veranda. Looking down, they saw in the shelter of the point a great raft with three little huts on it. The white tug-boat that had been towing it down river was tied up at the wharf. They could hardly keep still during prayers and breakfast, and the moment they were released they pulled on their coats and rushed down to the wharf, with Father, Oncle Édouard and several friends in their wake.

The storm had passed but it had taken the summer with it. The world looked tattered and torn, and it was very windy and cold and bleak. Scarcely a leaf was left on the trees and the garden was strewn with broken branches. The river was alive with white-caps, and on its far shore only a cold blue line divided grey sky from grey water.

As they went down, the wind blew so hard that they could hardly stand up. High waves broke over the wharf and spray hit their faces. The tug-boat tossed in the water, at one moment high above the wharf, at the next with only her bridge and funnel showing. Two or three men stood smoking on the wharf.

Father spoke to these men while the children strained to hear all they could about the raft. It had come down from Trois-Rivières. On it the crew had passed a dreadful night, fearing it would break up and they would all be drowned. Father told them that he and the children would like to visit it as soon as the weather improved. At that moment the captain appeared. He was a little man with bushy side whiskers and a cap just like the one worn by the *bateau* captain at the mill. He invited everyone aboard the tug-boat.

Boarding was a chancy affair because everything was wet and slippery. In rough weather a gangplank is either like a steep hill going up or like the other side of the hill going down. The children were frightened but ashamed to show their fear when the captain was so confident. When at last they were safely aboard, the captain showed them his own cabin, the galley, and the engine room. After that he offered the gentlemen a *petit coup* (which as you'll remember from Beau-Charles in Quebec was a drop of strong drink). Father thanked him and said they couldn't take anything so soon after breakfast.

Back at home Father said he thought it would be nice for the children to take a bag of apples to

the captain and his men. So they got a potato bag from *père* Beaudet and soon it was full to overflowing with windfalls from the storm. More were gathered up by the girls in their skirts and by the boys in their caps. Then Edmond and Alain hitched up their own mare Dolly to the *tombereau* — the farm cart — and drove down to the tug. The captain thanked

✦✦

them from the bottom of his heart and asked them to present his regards to their Father the Seigneur and Madame their mother. He and the mate stood on either side of the pile of apples as the boys drove away.

Next day the wind had gone down and the river was a dull grey sheet with little silver lines drawn across it where the sun broke through the clouds. Against the dark background of the far shore the church and houses of Cap-Santé stood out white and clear. Breakfast was just over when the captain and the mate, dressed in their best clothes, arrived to invite the whole family to visit the raft that afternoon.

Accordingly, at half-past twelve Beau-Charles rang the bell to call the children in for an early lunch. The bell was an old ship's bell which hung under the eaves, with a long rope that came down through an opening in the upstairs veranda. The rope was a great temptation to the children, each of whom had been spanked at one time or another for ringing it long before meal times.

After lunch the wagons and Mother's carriage came to the door, for the family always drove in style when paying a call, even when there was but a short way to go. It was a tight fit in the wagons and the children had to sit on each other's knees. The captain was waiting at the wharf at which a small boat stood ready to take them to the raft. Two trips were needed to take them all.

The children had never been on a raft before and found it strange and enchanting. It was like a flat island made of squared timbers instead of earth and grass. Single planks laid across the logs served as narrow streets leading to the three huts. You had to be very careful on the planks for fear of losing your balance and falling off. The huts were built of rough-hewn boards. The first was the kitchen, the second a storehouse for barrels of salt pork and all the odds and ends you need on a raft, and the third the men's dormitory.

Inside this last hut an iron stove stood in the middle, surrounded by bunks along the sides. Two men were in bed. As soon as the captain led the family in they climbed down to be presented. It was then that the visitors saw their flushed faces covered with red speckles. Mother asked what the matter was.

'I'm not sure,' replied the captain. 'It may be chickenpox or it may be smallpox. The two are so alike that it takes a doctor to tell them apart.'

Mother told him she hoped they would soon be well and hurried the family out of the hut. She thanked the captain and said they ought to be going

✦✦

home. The children showed their disappointment, as did the captain.

'Oh, madame! he said,' the cook has prepared a little *collation* – a snack – and I hope you will honour us by taking something.'

Before Mother could reply, Father appeared, and when the captain repeated his invitation he said they would be happy to stay. And so the raftsmen led the family into the kitchen hut which was prepared for anything but a light snack. A long table covered with oilcloth occupied the centre of the room, with benches drawn up on either side and a high stool for the captain at one end. On the table were a giant apple tart, heaping plates of doughnuts, and a layer cake with pink icing. Warming on the stove were pans of fried eggs ready for dishing out.

When the guests were seated the cooks brought plates of eggs and thick slices of bread and butter. Then they poured out mugs of tea from a huge enamel pot and handed round a bowl of brown sugar. None of the family except the boys had much appetite but the captain kept urging them on, saying '*Gênez-vous pas*' – don't be shy. So the family finished what was on their plates before saying their farewells and being rowed ashore.

Mother couldn't wait to get home. When Mary Ann was told about the sick men on the raft she made the children take off all their clothes, scrubbed them with carbolic soap, and put them into clean clothes. The rest of the day passed without incident and by morning everyone had forgotten the men with red spots.

But several mornings later Julie awoke with a bad headache and a sore throat. When she looked into the mirror she saw eyes as red as if she had been crying. With a start she remembered the raft and decided she had smallpox and was about to die. Feeling very sad but very important, she went to the nursery door and called Mary Ann, not wishing to go in for fear of infecting the other children. If they caught smallpox and died she would be to blame.

When Mary Ann came, Julie didn't exactly say she was dying. That was because she thought it would be more heroic to say nothing and let the others find out for themselves; and when they did, and were all weeping copiously, she would quietly tell them she had known it all along. Then she would ask them to kneel and pray for her as she gently expired just like the heroine in a book. But Mary Ann's response wasn't quite in line with Julie's romancing. 'O Holy

Mother!' she exclaimed, 'didn't I know you'd all go and get them dratted measles? Go back to bed, Miss Julie. I'll tell your ma.'

Nothing daunted, Julie got back into bed, lay flat on her back, pulled the bedclothes up under her chin, clasped her hands over her breast, and began preparing for death. Mother came in and then Father. Father joked about her face, saying it would soon look like a currant bush; Mother felt her hands and sent for the doctor. Julie looked at Father pityingly and thought how sad he would be when she was gone.

That was not to say that the grown-ups were complacent. They very well knew how quickly measles or chickenpox or mumps could spread through a family. So after much discussion it was decided that Tante Mathilde, Mary Ann, and the other children should leave the next day, as it was a Friday and the market boat would be going to Quebec. Mother would stay behind to nurse Julie.

Father, Oncle Édouard, and the visitors who had come for the shooting were also to stay. It was the end of Oncle Édouard's leave before he went back to India, and he wanted to spend his last fortnight at Platon. The children were sad at his leaving, but he consoled them by asking them what they would like him to bring from India next year. Both Edmond

and Alain coveted Indian scimitars. Ever since their uncle had first told them how a pukka warrior sliced off an enemy's head with one mighty swipe, they had been practising this bloodthirsty art as best they could with sticks. In the end Oncle Édouard had a long list of things and promised to do his best to find them. The only thing he couldn't guarantee was the baby elephant Mic wanted, but he offered to substitute a monkey.

Preparations for the children's departure set up a great bustle in the house. Everyone rushed to and fro gathering up the summer's treasures and doing the things that had been put off until now. Alain ran to the *boutique* to sharpen his knife, Edmond mended the minnow box, and Henri began building a hutch for his white mouse. The mouse he intended to take with him to town, but he knew that if Mary Ann got wind of it she would forbid him. His plan was to put the mouse in its hutch, hide it in the coach-house, and then at the last minute smuggle it on board ship where it wouldn't be noticed amongst all the luggage. Ethel tried to help him, because they always did things together, but Henri was so testy that she had to leave him to his own devices.

That whole day he was in fact so crochety, even with his beloved Beau-Charles, that as he was put to bed he kicked Mary Ann for getting soap in his eyes. By morning he had a headache, red eyes, and a runny nose. He too had the measles, which meant yet another change of plans. Mary Ann was now to stay behind to nurse him, as it would be too much for Mother to handle two invalids.

The ship was to leave at noon. At eleven there was a great tramping on the stairs as Narcisse and Cléophas hauled the trunks down. Tante Mathilde and the children who were well had a last picnic-style lunch in the dining room, and the carriages drove up to the door. Those who were leaving said their good-byes to Julie and Henri, and then came the sound of the carriages driving off, and at last the far-off whistle of the ship.

A great silence fell over Platon. The only sounds were the soft ra-ra-ra of *père* Beaudet raking up dry leaves and the hoarse cawing of the crows in the tree-tops. From her bed Julie could see the blue sky and the bare branches of trees, and the creeper threading its way through the fretwork of the veranda. Henri saw nothing at all because he was crying into his pillow over Mary Ann's refusal to let him have his mouse in the nursery.

Once the brother and sister became accustomed to being in bed, the time passed quickly. Henri made a scrap-book and Julie learned a whole chapter of the Bible by heart as well as the first part of 'The Lady of the Lake.' Soon they were quite well again.

Autumn was well on its way when Oncle Édouard and his guests left. The house felt emptier than ever. The only rooms still in use were Mother's sitting room, the nursery, the dining room, Father's study, and the room where he kept his guns and

cases of stuffed birds. The rest had their shutters
closed tight and their furniture covered with dust
sheets. Mother and Mary Ann busied themselves
with putting linen and silver away. With nothing else
to do, Julie and Henri spent most of their time out
of doors with Father. After lunch each day he would
take his gun and they would set off with his two
dogs Diana and Ray.

The woods were now all silver and grey, with
only a few crumpled red berries still clinging to the
bushes. In the sky the sun shone like a pale silver
disk. The bare fields were empty except for the
occasional ploughman and his horses. Sometimes on
their walks Father would raise his gun when a flock
of snowbirds whirred up from the furrows, and two
or three of the little white-breasted birds would flut-
ter to the ground. The dogs would dart off and come
trotting back to lay them at their master's feet. Father
would say, 'Good dog,' and Henri would gather up
the birds and carry them by their legs.

These were glorious days. But like all good
things they came to an end and it was time to follow
the rest of the family to town.

An Exciting End to the Summer

THE DAY ON WHICH FATHER, MOTHER, MARY Ann, Julie, and Henri left Platon for Quebec began very cold and still. A blue haze hung over the St Lawrence, hiding the opposite shore.

'There must be forest fires somewhere,' observed Cléophas as he drove them to the wharf. 'Look how thick the smoke is over the north shore.'

As this was to be the *Sainte-Marie*'s last trip of the season, the landing-stage was crowded. Sacks of potatoes were piled high upon each other, as were crates of chickens, ducks, and geese. There were whole pigs slit up the middle, sides of beef, and boxes of apples. Women sat on the boxes beside their goods and groups of men stood round talking.

The ship was a long time getting under way. But at four o'clock her whistle blew, her paddle wheels

✦✦✦

churned, and she moved into the river in a big semi-circle. The two Joly children and their mother stood on the narrow deck at the stern watching the long point of Platon slowly fade into the distance. They passed all the familiar places: the big shallow bay where they had minnowed and the little point where they had found the *Rancid Butter* that bright July morning. Then came the marshy shore where bullocks grazed and Father and Oncle Édouard had gone snipe shooting, and the beach where they had had their picnic suppers. On and on they went until at last Pointe-Platon was no more than a faint grey line.

Once the Seigneury disappeared from sight Father went to see the captain. When he returned he told the family, 'It will be eight o'clock before we get in. We had better have some supper and then

the children should have a nap. I shouldn't be surprised if we were a good deal later, with all this fog and smoke.'

The children's supper was in the cabin. As the window had to be shut to keep the oil lamp from blowing out, it became very hot and stuffy. When the plates and cups were stowed away, Mother put Julie into the lower berth and Henri into the upper. She and Father put on their coats and went out for a stroll while Mary Ann went off to talk to a friend in the public saloon.

Julie and Henri were soon asleep. But not for long. They woke to the noise of sailors tramping on the deck above, people talking in *Première Classe*, and the thud of the paddle wheels.

'Would you like me to read you a story?' Julie asked.

'Oh, yes!' cried Henri.

So Julie got up, found her book, and settled herself on a stool under the lamp. Henri climbed down to the lower berth. Julie had been reading to him for some time when there was a terrific crash. She was thrown off her stool and Henri against the wall of the berth. A moment later came sounds of people shrieking and running about, and then repeated short blasts on the ship's whistle. Julie's

✣✣✣

heart thumped. Catching Henri by the arm, she dragged him out of the berth.

'Hurry, hurry!' she cried. 'We must find Mamma and Papa.'

She opened the cabin door to see people rushing through the glass doors into the public saloon. She and Henri were carried along in the crowd until with gasps of relief they caught sight of Father.

'Papa, Papa!' she shouted.

He heard her and fought his way to them. Lifting Henri to his shoulder, he took Julie by the hand and ran along with the crowd to the bow. Here the deck was jammed with people. Women screamed, men shouted, and the whistle continued its staccato blasts. It was pitch black except for a single lantern on the mast. The crowd pushed past Father until quite suddenly the captain was beside him.

'We've struck a *bateau* loaded with wood,' he said. 'She has sunk but the wood is floating. I've already been down with a line and made a raft of the planks. All the passengers will be safe if only they stay calm. Speak to them, Monsieur Joly, speak to them!'

Father climbed up on a bench and shouted to the passengers, his voice rising above the whistle, the cries of women, and the splintering of timbers.

'Calm yourselves, my friends,' he cried. 'Take courage, trust in God and you will be saved. Only be calm and obey the captain.'

By then Mother had joined the family. She caught the children by the hand. 'Where is Mary Ann?' she asked. 'I don't know,' Father replied. 'I'll try to find out.'

Meanwhile the captain was fighting his way through the passengers, with the Jolys following after him. He led them to a part of the deck where they could look down into the dark river and see a faint red light rising and falling. Men were lowering planks towards this light. The captain leapt down into the night. His voice came up to them:

'Now come down one by one.'

'Don't be afraid,' said Father as he put Julie on a plank and let her slide down into the blackness. The captain caught her below. Henri came next.

'Hold tight to Henri,' Father shouted down to Julie. She took his hand and they stood shivering together on the raft as more people came slithering down. The two children could just make out the great rope that held their log raft close to the *Sainte-Marie*. All around them were the sounds of splitting timbers and the piteous cries of the passengers.

Above the din Father's strong voice came from above:

'Courage, my friends, courage!'

Then a steady stream of people began to slide down. The ship's deck was by now nearly level with the raft. The *Sainte-Marie* was sinking fast.

'Where's Mamma, where is she?' queried Henri between his sobs. Julie was crying too. Then from the deck the captain's voice rang out:

'I must cut the cable now, monsieur, so hurry, hurry!'

At last the children saw Mother coming down, and they stumbled to her over the logs. Last of all came Father and the captain. The line having been cut, the raft began to drift off rapidly into the darkness – but not too soon for them to see *Sainte-Marie's* bow rise high into the air, the light still burning on her mast, and then sink out of sight, leaving behind only her wreckage on the smoke-shrouded water.

'If only the ropes hold,' said the captain, 'and the raft doesn't fall apart, we shall have some hope of getting to shore.'

A poor horse swam up and tried three times to climb aboard. Twice he got his forelegs up on the logs, showing one white leg and a white streak down his face. The third time, a man had to hit him over the head with a board to prevent him from capsizing the raft. With a high-pitched scream he fell back into the river.

Women were on their knees praying aloud. To Julie their voices seemed to merge with the swish of the water, but every now and then she made out the Latin words *ora pro nobis* – 'pray for us.' Near them a man stood swaying back and forth, waving his arms and crying out, '*Priez, les créatures, priez*' – pray, you people, pray! Julie tried her best to pray for Mary Ann but she didn't know to pray for the dead – and she was pretty sure Mary Ann had perished.

Henri, too, was thinking of Mary Ann. He didn't want to be glad she was dead, but if she was he hoped Nanou would become their nurse. Nanou would let him keep his mouse.

Mother stood very still, holding the children's hands. She kept brushing away the tears from her face. Julie was awed because she had never seen a grown-up cry.

It was icy cold, and to make matters worse the spray swept up and drenched them. Father took off his coat and wrapped it round Henri and put his muffler round Julie, but even these didn't keep the chill out. After a while Henri's head dropped on his mother's knee and in spite of all he fell fast asleep. Julie stayed wide-awake, uncontrollably shivering.

At long last the first faint streaks of dawn appeared in the eastern sky, which gradually turned red and gold. Then, as daylight spread over the river in an even silvery grey, the people on the raft saw to their great relief that they had drifted quite close to shore. Houses and barns and a church spire came into view, and extending into the river was a wharf with a little shed at its extremity. Suddenly the raft came to a halt with a dull thud.

'We're aground!' said the captain. 'Can anyone swim?'

'I can,' answered Henri, waking up.

'Yes, I know,' said Father, 'but you must stay here and take care of Mamma and Julie. I'll go.' He rolled up his wet trousers above the knees and lowered himself over the edge. Down into the water he went until it was nearly up to his shoulders. 'It's not very deep,' he called out, 'and the tide is going out.'

'We'll come with you,' shouted several of the men.

'Two are enough,' said the captain. 'I may need the rest of you here if the raft begins to move.'

So the two men jumped in and waded with Father towards shore. They floundered a good deal,

because it's hard to stand upright when at any moment you may stumble over a submerged rock or sink into a deep pool. But at last they climbed up on the beach, shook themselves, and set out for the village. After that they were hidden by trees and houses, but those watching from the raft could hear a dog bark as they walked towards the village.

In no time men from the village were seen running to the beach and four carts were driving down at full tilt. One cart came to the wharf and deposited something there.

'It's a boat,' said the captain.

The children could see the villagers quite clearly now, dropping the boat into the river. Two got in and began to row. When they reached the raft the captain made the Jolys get in first, and then as many of the other women and children as the boat would hold. In all it took eight trips to bring all the

++

people to shore. They clambered into the carts and headed for the village.

Smoke had already begun to curl up from the chimneys, and women and children ran from their houses to see what all the excitement was. Halfway along the road the *curé* met the carts. He had been hurrying as fast as he could, but as he was short and fat he made less progress than his parishioners. He seized the Jolys' hands and said between gasps for breath, 'It's a miracle you've been saved. *Le bon Dieu* has been good to you, very good indeed!' And with that he blessed them with the sign of the cross.

He then took the family and the captain directly to the *presbytère* – the priest's house. The rest of the people were billeted in various cottages, for each householder was anxious to do something to help, and to hear about the wreck.

The priest's housekeeper had lit all the fires in the house and made a great steaming pot of coffee. The *curé* – the priest – took down a bottle from the cupboard in the *salon* and made each one take a small drink along with his coffee. Then the housekeeper took Mother, Julie, and Henri up to the best bedroom to take off their wet clothes. She brought an armful of her own clothes, telling Mother to use anything she and the children could wear, then bustled off to find dry clothes for the men.

The borrowed garments fitted Mother quite well and, with a great deal of pinning-up, Julie as well. But there was nothing whatsoever to fit poor little Henri. All Mother could find was a pair of the housekeeper's pink flannelette drawers. They were trimmed with lace and were far too big for him; and of course he felt absolutely miserable in them. But Mother told him it was only until his own clothes were dry. As soon as he and Julie were dressed she sent them down while she herself dressed.

The children found Father, the *curé*, and the captain in the *salon* smoking cigars and talking about the wreck. When the jolly round priest laid eyes on Henri he laughed so hard that he had to hold his sides. '*Regarde-lui donc*,' he cried, '*dire qu'à son âge, il est foutré dans les pantalons d'une vieille fille*' – just think of it! Him at his age dressed up in an old maid's bloomers! Father and the captain, wearing the dry clothes the housekeeper had found for them, smiled out of politeness to the *curé*, but this only made Henri the more miserable. It was a relief when the housekeeper came to tell them that breakfast was on the table.

✠✠✠

It was a delicious meal and tasted doubly good after the ordeal. When it was over, Father and the captain went off with the *curé* to see how the other people from the *Sainte-Marie* were faring. They were gone a long time, and when at last they came back Mother asked for any news of Mary Ann.

'None at all, my dear,' Father replied sadly. Julie began to weep. As for Henri, he was still thinking of Nanou. If she became their nurse he could slide down banisters, tear the knees of his stockings, and keep his mouse with never a scolding or a bother on the ear. But it seemed too good to be true, and as Mother and Julie were crying he thought it only proper to join in.

When the time came to catch the train to Quebec the housekeeper gave each member of the family another cup of coffee and a big slice of cake. They all thanked her warmly, and the *curé* drove them, all in their own dry clothes, to the station in his buggy.

A great many people from the wreck thronged the platform, all looking woebegone. Father, the captain, and the *curé* went among them trying to cheer them up. They had lost everything. The last farmers' market of the season was always an important one to which the country folk brought the winter provisions they had promised their customers: ducks and pigs, tubs of butter and apples as well as hares, partridges, and other wild game. All these had been lost in the river, and they would all be the poorer in the winter months.

The locomotive hissed to a stop. Everyone rushed to get aboard and find a seat, but it was clear that there wouldn't be room for all. At the rear of the train was a carriage no one got into, and to it Father led the family. A grand gentlemen with gold braid on his cap helped them on board. This carriage, called a parlour car, was very splendid — to the children's eyes more so than their drawing room at home. The seats were covered in red plush and there were looking glasses in gold frames between the windows. A porter in a white jacket showed them to their seats. There were only five other people in the carriage: two ladies and three gentlemen reading newspapers. Hardly had the Jolys sat down when one gentleman laid down his paper and came to shake hands with Mother. He was astonished to hear of the wreck, as were the other passengers and the porter who gathered round. So absorbed were they all that no one noticed Father's return; and so he was made to tell the story all over again.

When at last the other passengers went back to

✠✠

their seats, and the children settled into theirs, Mother asked Father for any further news of Mary Ann.

'I am afraid there is none, my dear,' he replied, holding her hand as she dabbed her eyes with her handkerchief. Father looked as sad as when Constable O'Rourke had come to take Beau-Charles away so many months ago. But the children's attention was diverted when a boy came through the carriage with a basket of oranges, bananas, and bars of chocolate. They hoped Father would buy them something but he didn't even notice the boy.

It was dark night when they arrived in Quebec, and bitterly cold as they got down from the train. But there, standing on the platform, were Edmond and Alain with an uncle and aunt, all beating their arms to keep warm. As they all hugged one another, Julie heard Alain say, 'Mary Ann's been crying her eyes out. She can't believe you're safe.'

'Mary Ann!' cried Father and Mother in unison. 'We thought she had been drowned.'

'No, she's all right,' said Alain. 'She floated down the river on a crate of hens. A ship picked her up early this morning above Cap-Rouge.'

A big tear rolled down Henri's cheek. As they walked along the station platform the tears came thick and fast. He was tired and cold and hungry. He'd had a terrible night and day, waking up on the raft soaked to the skin and then having to put on the pink drawers, and now hearing that Mary Ann was alive and waiting for him at home. It was the last straw. His hopes of keeping the white mouse were dashed.

Outside the station the rockaway stood waiting. Narcisse leapt down and shook hands over and over, exclaiming, '*Mais que le bon Dieu a été bon pour nous*!' – how good the Lord has been to us. Then they drove off through the dark streets where, as ever, the gas lamps shone like yellow moons. Up and up they climbed, because the station is at the lowest level of the city and their house nearly at the highest, until at last they were at their own door. When it opened, a welcoming light was cast on the pavement. Tante Mathilde, Tilly, Mic, Mary Ann, and all the rest of the household ran out to greet them.

Mary Ann caught Julie and Henri up in her arms. 'Ah, my precious lambs,' she cried, 'I never thought I'd set eyes on either of you again!'

Everyone talked excitedly on the way in. Supper was ready in the dining room, and they sat round the table any which way, just as at a picnic. As Beau-Charles served the soup to Mother, he said, 'I have made a vow to the Blessed Virgin, madame, that if you were saved I'd never again take a *petit coup*, not even on my wedding day.'

'I am glad to hear that,' replied Mother drily. But the children feared that if he never had another little dram they would never again get one of his delicious cakes with *Pardon* written on its icing.

Mother turned to Mary Ann. 'Sit down,' she said, 'and tell us all that happened to you.'

So Mary Ann described how she had been sitting in the public saloon with her friend when she felt the *Sainte-Marie* colliding with the *bateau*. She had run back to *Première Classe* to find the children but had to fight her way against so many people rushing in the opposite direction that when she reached the first-class saloon the water was already spreading across the floor. Wading to the Jolys' cabin

she found the door jammed, and when she got it open the cabin was empty. By that time the water was so deep in the saloon that she had to climb out through a window to the narrow deck outside. Then, because the deck was nearly at water level, she tried to clamber up to the top of the ship but lost her balance and fell into the river. The next thing she knew, she was clutching something that turned out to be the crate of hens. Somehow she managed to pull herself on top of it and cling to it as it drifted down river.

For the first few minutes she heard people's voices, but they faded away and very soon the *Sainte-*

++

Marie was far behind and sinking fast. She thought the family had gone down with the ship. All night long she clung to the crate with hands that became numb with cold. At dawn she spied the smoke of a steamer far in the distance. This steamer grew larger and larger until she could make out people like specks moving about on deck. She wriggled out of her coat and waved it frantically. By a miracle the ship began to slow down and she saw a boat being lowered over the side and men scrambling into it. She knew then that she had been spotted and would be rescued.

'Oh, m'm,' she concluded, 'them sea captains are grand men. I always was against the sea as you know, m'm, but if ever the good Lord wills that I'm to marry I'll ask him to make it to a captain.'

'Well, Mary Ann,' said Father, 'we shall drink to you and the lucky man who gets you.' He passed the decanter of port, raised his glass and said, 'Here's to your good health and that of your captain!' Everyone stood up for the toast. Tears ran down Mary Ann's cheek as she replied, 'Thank you kindly, sir, but may the good Lord keep me from marriage at my time of life, even to a sea captain.'

Mother told the children it was high time they were in bed after such a long and eventful day. As

Mary Ann scrubbed Henri's face he asked her if he could have his white mouse here in town.

'Now Henri,' she replied, 'if you start pestering me about that varmint of yours I'll warm your pelt for good, I will. But,' she added as an afterthought, 'if Narcisse allows it in the stable you can keep it. I won't have it in the nursery.' And as she tucked him in and kissed him good-night she said, 'You'll find something nice under your pillow.'

He slipped his hand under the pillow and there was a peppermint bull's-eye. Blissfully he popped it into his mouth and could hear the faint noises of Tilly, Mic, and Ethel enjoying theirs too. He was happy as he cuddled in his warm bed because he was sure Narcisse would let him keep the mouse in the stable. Perhaps after all it was better to have Mary Ann as nurse than Nanou because she knew all the things he liked best, especially bulls'-eyes.

He fell asleep at once and dreamed that he and the mouse were together in the nursery and had made a nest under the bed. Mary Ann came in with a big broom and tried to sweep them out – but suddenly she turned into a huge red and white bull's-eye. He knew it was Mary Ann, though, because the bull's-eye kept saying, 'I'll warm your pelt for you!'

✲✲✲✲✲✲✲✲✲✲✲✲✲✲✲✲✲✲✲✲✲✲✲✲✲✲✲✲✲✲✲✲✲✲✲✲✲✲✲

Somehow the mouse turned into a dark river which said in Beau-Charles' voice, '*Pardonnez-moi, pardonnez-moi.*'

And then suddenly it was morning, and Mary Ann was pulling back the bedclothes and saying. 'Wake up, lazy-bones!'

It was another day.

THE END